MACMILLAN MASTER GUIDES

VOLPONE

BY BEN JONSON

MICHAEL STOUT

MACMILLAN

First published 1988 by
THE MACMILLAN PRESS LTD
Houndmills, Basingstoke, Hampshire RG21 2XS
and London
Companies and representatives
throughout the world

ISBN 0–333–42166–3

A catalogue record for this book is available
from the British Library.

Printed in China

Reprinted 1993

To my family

CONTENTS

ACKNOWLEDGEMENTS

Cover acknowledgement: Portrait of *Ben Jonson*, after Abraham van Blyenbirch

1 BEN JONSON LIFE AND BACKGROUND

Ben Jonson was born in 1572, a month after the death of his clergyman father. His mother subsequently married a master bricklayer. Jonson was a pupil at Westminster School where he received an education in the classics under William Camden and developed a passion for scholarship which lasted all his life. He later acknowledged his debt to his old headmaster in an epigram addressed to him, which stated:

> Camden, most reverend head, to whom I owe
> All that I am in arts, all that I know.

The revival of interest in classical literature was one of the most important features of Renaissance humanism and a grammar school boy of Jonson's time would have received a thorough education in ancient Greek and Latin. This grounding in the classics influenced all his writing, which is full of borrowings from and allusions to Greek and Roman literature. *Volpone* was influenced by the comedies of Aristophanes, by Roman comedy, by the satires of Juvenal, and the song addressed to Celia by Volpone was adapted from a lyric by Catullus.

The future playwright did not continue his education at university as he might have expected to do, but was forced to work for his stepfather as an apprentice bricklayer after leaving Westminster School at the age of seventeen in 1589. He did not enjoy this experience and volunteered to fight in Flanders. Later he claimed to have challenged and killed one of the enemy in hand to hand combat, stripping him of his weapons and armour. He was married to Anne Lewis in 1594 but the marriage was not a particularly happy one, for he later described his wife as 'a shrew but honest'. They had two children who died in infancy. Jonson felt their loss keenly and mourned them in epitaphs. A third child, a son, died two years before his father.

He began his theatrical career as an actor with a group of strolling players. In 1597 he completed the play *The Isle of Dogs*, which had been started by Thomas Nashe. This is the first recorded instance of his play writing and it was commissioned by Philip Henslowe for his company. Because of the play's content, the dramatist was jailed for sedition and all copies of the play were destroyed. This was the first of many scrapes with the law. He was released from Marshalsea prison after only two weeks. (Jonson later expressed a highly criticial attitude to the law, and to lawyers in particular, in *Volpone*.) His most serious brush with the law came in 1597 when he killed fellow actor Gabriel Spencer in a duel. He was imprisoned in Newgate for manslaughter and only escaped execution by claiming benefit of clergy. This was an ancient legal right, previously enjoyed by the clergy, but later extended to those who could prove they could read, by which they were exempt from the death penalty. Jonson was branded on the thumb (a mark which stayed with him all his life), all his possessions were confiscated, and he was released.

During his time in prison he was converted to Roman Catholicism. This was not a judicious move at the time because of the legislation aimed specifically at Catholics. They were forbidden to take degrees at Oxford and Cambridge unless they first took the oath recognising the supremacy of the Crown in matters of religion, and were discriminated against in other ways in public life. In addition, Catholics were viewed with extreme suspicion in Protestant England, and were considered a subversive influence. Anti-Catholic hysteria reached a climax after the Gunpowder Plot of 1605 (an event hinted at in *Volpone*), just one year before the play's first performance. Jonson and his wife were charged with recusancy in 1606, (refusing to attend their local parish church). In 1610 he prudently returned to the Church of England.

Shakespeare knew Ben Jonson and acted in his play *Every Man in His Humour* when it was performed by the Lord Chamberlain's Company in 1598. In the following year *Every Man Out of His Humour* appeared at the Globe. He followed this with *Cynthia's Revels*, (1600), and *The Poetaster* (1601), which poked fun at the style of Marston and initiated the 'War of the Theatres' in which Jonson and his contemporary playwrights mocked each other in their plays. Dekker's play *Satiromastix* was an answer to Jonson and ridiculed both Jonson, in the figure of Horace, and his friend, the poet Drayton. The first of his surviving tragedies *Sejanus* was acted in 1603 by Shakespeare's company at the Globe. (The tragedies were not popular at the time and are rated less highly by modern critics than his comedies.)

From this time on most of the playwright's income derived from the masques he wrote for King James and his court, starting with the *Masque of Blackness* performed in 1605. From the beginning of his reign James aroused the antagonism of the House of Commons with his belief in the superior rights of the king over the Commons. This conflict was the major constitutional crisis of the time and was eventually to lead to the English Revolution, when his son Charles I was overthrown and executed by the victorious Parliamentarians. In his dealings with Parliament James arrogantly insisted on the divine right of kings. The masque was a genre which reinforced this exalted concept of the godlike and God-given powers of the King. The King and his Court actually appeared in their semi-divine roles.

Masques were presented at Court and not to a public audience. Their cost was enormous as they called for elaborate sets, complex stage machinery and exotic costumes, all of which were designed by Jonson's collaborator, Inigo Jones. They attracted a great deal of criticism from those outside the Court on grounds of extravagance and they were also criticised on grounds of immorality. Inigo Jones's costumes for the female characters in the *Masque of Blackness* were considered too revealing. Masques also increased antagonism towards the monarchy because of their ideology of the divine authority of the King, and because they exemplified Court culture, which was not shared by the rest of the country. This gulf between Court and country was one of the causes of the English Revolution.

Despite his humble social background, Ben Jonson must be considered pro-monarchy and a conservative in his active support of Stuart political ideology. In his plays he frequently attacks the rising merchant class, but in *Volpone* itself the one unqualified hero is Peregrine, who is described as a traveller, while Sir Politic Would-Be, who is a knight, is ridiculed as a fool. We must therefore beware of over-simplifying his beliefs. It seems likely that the dramatist had his audience in mind, and for a Court audience, which he would have had for his masques, was quite happy to provide support for the monarchy, while in his citizen comedies, which were performed in the public theatres, his subject matter was often the citizens and city of London, where opposition to the monarchy centred.

Ben Jonson and Inigo Jones were collaborators and rivals for the next twenty-five years in the court masques. Jonson quarrelled with Inigo Jones and, although originally they fell out over whose name should appear first on the title pages of the court masques on which they collaborated, he also believed that the words were more important than the visual elements. He wrote a long poem 'An Expostulation with Inigo Jones' in which he derided Jones's contribution to the masque. Jonson's particular original contribution was to invent the anti-masque which preceded the masque and added drama and variety to what was in essence a static and formal glorification of the monarchy.

In 1605 the dramatist was in prison again for his part in writing *Eastward Ho!* His two collaborators Marston and Dekker were gaoled and he volunteered to join them. The play mocked the Scots, and King James, who was Scottish himself, was not amused. They were all shortly released. *Volpone* was first performed in 1606 at the Globe Theatre and then at Oxford and Cambridge. Jonson specifically dedicates the play to the two universities in his epistle to the play in the edition printed in 1607. His dramatic career continued with *The Silent Woman*, performed at Whitefriars Theatre in 1609. This was followed by *The Alchemist* in 1610 at the Globe. *Bartholomew Fair* appeared at the Hope Theatre in 1614, and in 1616 *The Devil is an Ass* at Blackfriars.

Unlike most of the dramatists of his time Jonson ensured that his works were published. It is obvious that he took his own writing seriously and expected others to do the same. Most of his plays appeared in book form shortly after their first performance. In 1616 he took the unusual step of publishing nine of his plays, two collections of his poetry and several masques in one volume: a folio entitled *The Works of Benjamin Jonson*. Although his supposed pretentiousness was mocked by some of his fellow writers, the publication of the folio established him as the foremost man of letters in England and King James awarded him a pension which was paid for the rest of his life.

In 1618 Jonson undertook a walking tour to Scotland. While there he stayed with William Drummond who recorded their conversations together. *Conversations with Drummond* provides us with a character portrait of the playwright as well as a record of some of his remarks and facts about his personal life which we would not otherwise know. In 1619 he received an honorary degree from Oxford University which must have pleased him. Ben Jonson had a capacity for friendship as well as for making enemies. His wide circle of friends included the poet and dean of St Paul's, John Donne, who wrote some verses in Latin commending *Volpone*. A group of loyal younger friends who called themselves 'the Sons of Ben', included the Cavalier poets Robert Herrick and Thomas Carew. In 1603 Jonson formed the Mermaid Club which met for conversation and to drink the wine for which the Mermaid Tavern was famous.

In 1623 Jonson's library was destroyed by fire and in the same year he paid tribute to Shakespeare in the Folio edition of Shakespeare's plays: 'To the Memory of My Beloved, the Author Mr. William Shakespeare: And What He Hath Left Us.' Charles I came to the throne in 1625 and Jonson and Inigo Jones collaborated in ever more lavish masques until they fell out and the dramatist ceased to write them. Today we tend to think of Charles I as a great patron of the arts, but the growing opposition to him did not see it that way. The building of the Banqueting House under James I, and its ornate decoration under Charles, as well as the exorbitant expense of the masques that were held there, increased criticism of the king and his Court. The gulf between Court and country widened ominously.

One of the later masques, *Pleasure Reconciled to Virtue*, influenced the young John Milton, gave him the name, and suggested the character of Comus, for his *Masque presented at Ludlow Castle*, performed in 1634. Jonson's last three plays, written for the public theatre were all comedies: *The Staple of News* (1625), *The New Inn* (1629), and *The Magnetic Lady* (1632), and did not enjoy a great deal of success. His misfortunes were added to in 1628 when he was paralysed by a stroke which confined him to his chambers. However, he was constantly visited by the 'Sons of Ben'. He continued writing up to the end and died on 6 August 1637 aged 65. He received a public funeral in Westminster Abbey which was attended by most of the nobility and gentry in London, and was laid to rest under the epitaph 'O rare Ben Jonson'.

Ben Jonson's writing career spanned the reigns of Elizabeth I, James I and Charles I. His literary production started in the High Renaissance of Elizabeth and continued through the Jacobean and up to the Cavalier period. He wrote plays, poetry and masques as well as a prose work, *Timber*, containing his thoughts about literature. He was a consciously didactic artist, whose influence by the classical authors, as well as his sense of himself as a public poet and his use of satire, point forward to the direction English poetry would take with Dryden and Pope. He was a contemporary of Shakespeare, influenced Milton, and must be rated next to these two giants in the literature of his time.

2 JONSONIAN COMEDY

2.1 HUMOURS

One of the first things that strikes the reader of Ben Jonson's comedies is that the characters do not develop in the way that Shakespeare's characters do. They tend to remain fixed throughout the course of the play in their dominant impulses. The only character in *Volpone* who evolves to a deeper understanding of himself, and swears he will adopt more prudent behaviour in the future, is Sir Politic Would-Be, in the sub-plot. All the main characters in Volpone are the same at the end of the play as they were at the beginning. They have achieved little increased insight into themselves or their condition. This is no reason for adverse criticism of Jonson's knowledge of human psychology. Indeed, in comedy some of the most amusing effects arise from characters behaving in a predictable way.

Jonson's characters are based on a different science of the mind from that with which we are familiar today. His concept of human psychology was essentially medieval and was derived from the theory of the humours which was commonly believed both in classical times and the Middle Ages. The word 'humour' was derived from Old French and Latin and was applied in medieval physiology to the four cardinal humours of the body which were supposed to determine a person's temperament: blood, phlegm, choler and melancholy. The dominance of any one humour predisposed a man's temperament in a particular direction. The playwright's concept of the part played by 'humour' may be judged from his comments on it in the prologue to *Every Man Out of His Humour*. It is clear that the meaning of the word 'humour' was changing at the time. In fact, he felt it necessary to define it in the figure of Asper.

> ASPER   The choler, melancholy, phlegm and blood,
> By reason that they flow continually

In some one part, and are not continent,
Receive the name of humours. Now thus far
It may, by metaphor, apply itself
Unto the general disposition:
As when some one peculiar quality
Doth so possess a man, that it doth draw
All his affects, his spirits, and his powers,
In their confluctions, all to run one way,
This may be truly said to be a humour. (99–109)

But for Jonson, on the whole, the word seems to have had negative connotations, as we can gather from *Every Man In His Humour* where two of the characters are discussing 'humour':

COB   Humour? . . . what is this humour? it's some rare thing I warrant.
PISO   Marry, I'll tell thee what it is (as 'tis generally received in these days): it is a monster bred in a man by self-love and affectation and fed by folly. (III. i. 132–5)

In *Volpone* Sir Politic and Lady Would-Be conform closely in their characterisation to this conception of humour.

2.2 DIDACTIC AND MORAL PURPOSE

Jonson believed in the didactic and moral purpose of his comedy, and considered it had a public function to correct behaviour. He expressed this belief both in the prologues to some of his comedies as well as through the voices of his characters, as in the Prologue to *Every Man Out of His Humour*, where the dramatist himself appears as the character Asper:

CORDATUS   . . . now if an idiot
Have but an apish or fantastic strain,
It is his humour.
ASPER   Well, I will scourge those apes,
And to these courteous eyes oppose a mirror,
As large as is the stage whereon we act;
Where they shall see the time's deformity
Anatomised in every nerve, and sinew,
With constant courage and contempt of fear. (115–22)

But he was not content merely to attack human folly, he also intended to expose vice:

ASPER   . . . my strict hand
Was made to seize on vice . . . (143–4)

He also saw his function as curative:

ASPER   And therefore I would give them pills to purge,
And make them fit for fair societies. (175–6)

By the time he came to write *Volpone* Jonson's tone of moral seriousness had deepened, and he moved on to expose serious vices: greed in particular. The playwright's clearest statement of his belief in the moral purpose and 'function' of the poet occurs in the Epistle to *Volpone*:

> For, if men will impartially, and not asquint, look toward the offices and function of a poet, they will easily conclude to themselves the impossibility of any man's being the good poet, without first being a good man. He that is said to be able to inform young men to all great virtues, keep old men in their best and supreme state . . . that comes forth the interpreter and arbiter of nature, a teacher of things no less than human, a master in manners; and can alone (or with a few) effect the business of mankind . . .
>   . . . and last the doctrine, which is the principal end of poesy: to inform men in the best reason of living . . .

But he also believed that comedy should make the audience laugh and he concludes the Prologue to *Volpone*:

> Only a little salt remaineth,
> Wherewith he'll rub your cheeks, till red with laughter,
> They shall look fresh a week after. (34–6)

He took the trouble to write a lengthy epistle and prologue to *Volpone* in which he expressed his intention to both instruct and entertain his audience. According to the critic Coburn Gum he was influenced in this by the example of Aristophanes, who also addressed the audience directly with his views in prefaces to his plays known as parabases.

2.3 THE UNITIES

In the Prologue to *Every Man Out of His Humour* there is a conversation between Cordatus and Mitis about satire and the laws of comedy which indicates Jonson's attitude to following the Unities of classical drama. During this discussion, Cordatus, who represents the playwright and expresses his views on the matter, describes the development of comedy from the Greeks to the Romans. In particular he describes how the various writers adapted it to their own purpose, and concludes by saying:

> I see not then but we should enjoy the same license, or free power to illustrate and heighten our invention, as they did; and not be tied to those strict and regular forms which the niceness of a few, who are nothing but form, would thrust upon us. (266–70)

He sees the classical unities and forms as something which he and his contemporaries should have the right to alter or adapt as they see fit. The Unities were derived from Aristotle's *Poetics* by Italian critics of the sixteenth century. The main three unities that the dramatist was supposed to observe were the unities of time, place and action. It must be remembered that Aristotle was attempting to describe the Ancient Greek tragedies of such writers as Sophocles which he had seen performed in the third century BC. These dramas were products of a very different historical and cultural environment from that of seventeenth-century England. To apply such statements rigidly to the drama of a different epoch was inappropriate and, as Jonson himself said, restricting.

With his background and reading in the classics he was well aware of the working methods of Greek and Roman dramatists, but did not allow such considerations to limit *Volpone* unduly, as he states in the Prologue to the play, speaking of himself in the third person:

> The laws of time, place, persons he observeth,
> From no *needful* rule, he swerveth. (31–2)

Thus Jonson, like Shakespeare, felt no need to follow slavishly the academic formulae employed by neo-classical critics as a dogmatic and prescriptive instrument of criticism. In particular, he deviates from the Unities by introducing a sub-plot. He was certainly influenced by classical writers of comedy such as Aristophanes, Plautus and Terence but used them as a starting point to develop his own brand of comedy which, although satirising vice, never failed to amuse and entertain his audience.

2.4 JONSON'S SCATOLOGICAL JOKES

One problem that faces the modern reader of *Volpone* is the large number of jokes that would be judged prurient by our twentieth-century standards, though not by Jonson's original audience.

Shakespeare's plays are full of jokes based on double meanings, usually of a sexual nature. The problem with Jonson is that many of his jokes and puns are based on excretory functions, what we would call today 'lavatory humour'. The Ancient Greek dramatist Aristophanes, who was a major influence on him, was also fond of this kind of humour. In his defence we can say that he was writing in an age that was less inhibited than our own. The jokes and puns are part of the work and to ignore them is to refuse to understand Jonson as he intended to be understood.

2.5 THE COMIC WORLD OF VOLPONE

In *Volpone* he creates an imaginary world where, initially, the professed standards of civilisation do not apply. Gold is worshipped as a god and greed is the most visible human emotion. The playwright reduces his characters to the level of animals. The suitors are as avaricious as birds of prey and Volpone himself is as crafty as a fox. In creating a world where emotions which are normally hidden are clearly on display, Jonson not only subverts civilised standards but makes an ironic commentary on their pretentiousness. The comic world of *Volpone* has an inner consistency and an inner logic which the audience accepts until the very end of the play, when normal civilised standards are restored, and the innocent are rewarded and the guilty punished.

The force of the comedy, as in many comedies, lies in the audience's recognition of the perverted nature of the values which are presented to them, and laughing at them, thus obtaining a sense of release. Jonson's intentions are therefore primarily satirical. Comedy is also valuable in releasing us, momentarily, from the intolerable pressures of civilisation. It reveals the unconscious thoughts and feelings upon whose repression civilisation depends in an unthreatening way, and discharges them harmlessly in laughter. Critics who have attacked the play for its so-called lack of 'morality' have not really observed how the comedy of *Volpone* functions.

3 SYNOPSIS AND SCENE-BY-SCENE SUMMARY AND COMMENTARY

3.1 SYNOPSIS

Volpone is an old and wealthy Venetian nobleman who worships gold. He has no children or relatives and maintains an unnatural household made up of a dwarf, a hermaphrodite, a eunuch, and a parasite called Mosca. Volpone and Mosca conspire together to defraud greedy legacy hunters. The three main would-be heirs are Voltore an advocate, Corvino a merchant, and Corbaccio, an old gentleman. Volpone pretends to be bedridden and mortally ill, while Mosca raises their hopes, in turn, of becoming his sole heir. As a result they attempt to outdo each other in the magnificence of their presents to him.

Mosca informs his master that Corvino has an extremely beautiful wife. Volpone determines to see her and disguises himself as the mountebank Scoto of Mantua in order to do so. When he sets eyes on Celia he is filled with desire, and begs Mosca to procure her for him. Mosca manages to persuade Corvino that by lending his wife, Volpone's health will be restored and he will name Corvino as his heir. Mosca has previously persuaded Corbaccio to disinherit his son Bonario in favour of Volpone, and now he brings Bonario to Volpone's house to overhear his father disown him, and hides him, unbeknown to his master. Corvino conveys Celia to Volpone and tells her that in order to rescue his finances she must go to bed with him, but she refuses. Celia is left alone with the invalid who attempts to seduce her and when this fails, tries to rape her. Unknown to Volpone, Bonario overhears everything, leaps out, accuses him of being an impostor, and rescues Celia.

When Corbaccio arrives, Mosca tells him the lie that Bonario, having learnt of his father's plan to disinherit him, has been looking for him with drawn sword, vowing to kill both him and Volpone. Outraged, Corbaccio says that this act shall indeed disinherit him and hands Mosca his will naming Volpone as his sole heir. In order to prevent Volpone's exposure by Bonario Mosca persuades Corvino and Corbaccio to make false accusations in court against both Celia and Bonario. Voltore, who is their advocate, accuses Celia of having an affair with Bonario and says that they were caught in the act by her husband Corvino, who has forgiven her; when Bonario's father Corbaccio heard of this he decided to disinherit his son; on the day that he was to be disinherited, Bonario with Celia entered Volpone's house, intending to murder Corbaccio and, not finding his father, he dragged the patient from his bed and tried to prevent his father making Volpone his heir by accusing him of attempted rape. Corvino and Corbaccio back up these allegations and, swayed by Voltore's eloquence, the magistrates order Celia and Bonario to be taken into custody.

Volpone now overreaches himself in his wish to vex the fortune hunters. He gives out that he is dead, names Mosca as his sole heir, and dresses him in a nobleman's gown. When the fortune hunters arrive, drawn by news of his death, they are infuriated to discover that Mosca has apparently outwitted them and is the heir. Volpone observes all this from a place of concealment. Next, Volpone in the disguise of a court official, and Mosca in his nobleman's clothes, go about the streets to torment the would-be heirs further.

Celia and Bonario are brought to the court for sentencing. Now that Voltore believes Mosca to be the heir, he is determined to be revenged on him, so he tells the court that Mosca is behind everything, and that Celia and Bonario are innocent. Volpone enters in his disguise of officer of the court and whispers to Voltore, who does not recognise him, that Volpone is still alive and that he is still the heir. Encouraged by him the advocate pretends to have a fit of madness, and says that his previous statement was false.

Mosca is sent for and Volpone, still in disguise, tells him to inform the court that his master is alive. Mosca first pretends that he does not recognise his patron, and asks him in an aside for half of what he owns. Volpone at first refuses and then agrees. Mosca maintains his pretence of not knowing who he is and tells Volpone he will not settle so cheaply now. The magistrates give the order for Volpone to be whipped for insolence – they still do not know who he is. He now realises that not only has he lost everything to Mosca, but that he will also suffer the humiliation of a public whipping. Determined that Mosca will not benefit from his downfall, he throws off his disguise and identifies himself to the court. In addition Volpone reveals the whole conspiracy, as he wants all his victims to suffer with him.

The court frees Celia and Bonario. It sentences Mosca to be whipped and to spend the rest of his life as a galley-slave. Volpone has all his property confiscated and is to be confined in chains until he is sick indeed. Voltore is banished from Venice and the legal profession. Corbaccio is to be confined to a monastery and his whole estate is to be given to his son Bonario, while Corvino is to suffer public humiliation and has to return Celia to her father with her dowry trebled.

The sub-plot, which counterpoints the main plot in a comic way, involves an eccentric and foolish English traveller, Sir Politic Would-Be, and his garrulous and pretentious wife, who is one of the legacy hunters. Peregrine, a younger and wiser man, tries to bring Sir Politic to his senses by playing a practical joke on him; and pretends that Sir Politic is to be arrested by the Venetian authorities as a spy. Sir Politic realises his gullibility, and decides to leave Venice with his wife, never to return.

3.2 SUMMARY AND COMMENTARY

Act I, Scene i

Summary

The play opens in Volpone's house. Volpone and Mosca enter, and Volpone addresses a hymn of praise to his gold. He boasts to Mosca that he does not get rich in a commonplace way and, flattering him, Mosca observes that he enjoys his wealth, and also gives some of it to him, and to the rest of his household. Volpone gives him money and Mosca goes out. Left by himself, Volpone reveals in a soliloquy that he gains his wealth by playing on the hopes of fortune hunters, who make presents to him, in the expectation of inheriting his future after his death.

Commentary

The opening speech of the play introduces us to Volpone's monomania, and the audience is immediately plunged into his unnatural world, where gold is worshipped like a god or saint. Jonson attempts both to shock the audience and to indicate how Volpone is to be perceived. Greed is a common human weakness, but by raising it to the level of a religion Volpone makes himself ridiculous. The first speech of the play indicates that Jonson is satirising Volpone his gross materialism, and his inversion of normal human values. It also prepares the audience for the main theme of the play, the way in which the exaggerated desire for wealth becomes an obsession, overriding all other considerations.

By the sheer force and verve of Jonson's writing, and the dynamism of the opening speech, the audience is compelled to accept the reality of Volpone's world, which is like a mirror image of the real one, with all the normal values reversed. In everyday life such impulses are hidden and concealed from others. But by bringing them out into the open and placing them centre stage, Jonson forces us to confront them. The effect of Volpone's self-dramatising speech on an audience is electrifying and it is one of the masterpieces of Jonson's oeuvre.

In his conversation with Mosca, where he boasts of the way he makes his financial gains, there are numerous references to capitalism and industry:

> VOLPONE   . . . since I gain
> No common way: I use no trade, no venture;
> I wound no earth with ploughshares; fat no beasts
> To feed the shambles; have no mills for iron,
> Oil, corn, or men, to grind 'em into powder;
> I blow no subtle glass; expose no ships
> To threat'nings of the furrow-faced sea;
> I turn no money in the public bank.
> Nor usure private . . . (39–40)

Despite Volpone's protestation that his hands are clean, the audience is left in no doubt as to his avarice and materialism, since the whole tone of the scene is one of praise for acquisition.

Mosca's comments reveal that Volpone is no simple miser; he enjoys the pleasures of the senses and also keeps an unnatural family:

> MOSCA   You will not lie in straw, whilst moths and worms
> Feed on your sumptuous hangings and soft beds,
> You know the use of riches, and dare give, now,
> From that bright heap, to me your poor observer,
> Or to your dwarf, or your hermaphrodite,
> Your eunuch, or what other household trifle.
> Your pleasure allows maintenance . . . (65–6)

Volpone is childless and the mock family he has created around himself is unnatural and unhealthy. His natural instincts have been replaced by unnatural ones. The dwarf, hermaphrodite and eunuch are an external representation of his perverted values.

In the final speech of the scene Jonson tells us that Volpone is a voluptuary and feels free to indulge himself in all the delights his fortune can buy. Throughout the scene there have also been many references to the purchasing power of gold. This indicates to the reader that material values prevail over human ones. Volpone is also ironical about the greed he arouses in the hearts of the would-be heirs, who hope to profit from his death, and compete with each other in the extravagance of the gifts they bring him. It is apparent that he plays on their weakness and greed, and thus enriches himself.

Act I, Scene ii

Summary
Mosca enters in company with Nano, Androgyno and Castrone, who comprise Volpone's unnatural household. They proceed to entertain Volpone with a short interlude which is concerned with the transmigration of the soul of Apollo through various incarnations to its present one, that of the body of Androgyno. This foolish entertainment pleases him, and he congratulates Mosca on it. There is a knock on the door and Volpone orders his household out. Mosca tells him that his visitor is Voltore the advocate and, in response, Volpone orders Mosca to bring him the clothes for his sick bed, and asks Voltore to wait. Mosca returns with the information that Voltore has brought him a large piece of plate. Volpone tells him to bring the visitor in, feigns illness, and when he hears Voltore's footsteps begins to groan.

Commentary
The decadence of Volpone's household is made even more explicit, with the appearance of Nano, Androgyno and Castrone to entertain him. Their names in Italian mean dwarf, hermaphrodite, and eunuch. The interlude they perform, created by Mosca, shows the transmigration of the soul of Apollo through various characters of antiquity to Pythagoras, descending through kings to fools, then through assorted members of the animal kingdom to its present grotesque resting place, Androgyno. The point of this is to show the gradual descent of a noble soul to the animal, and then beneath the animal to the hermaphrodite, thus indicating the debased values which prevail in Volpone's household and, by implication, in Volpone himself.

Their performance concludes with a song in praise of fools which includes the puns on 'bauble', which could also mean penis, and 'stool' which even today means excrement. The song ends with the final pun: 'Hee, hee, hee?', which represents their childish laughter as well as the third person pronoun. Jonson delights in puns and word-play. The entertainment is brought to an end by the sudden knocking of Voltore, one of the suitors for Volpone's wealth. The name 'Voltore' indicates his nature: it is Italian for vulture. Volpone immediately prepares himself to feign sickness and takes to his bed. He refers to the legacy hunters as: 'vulture, kite, raven and gor-crow, all my birds of prey'. The audience is thus encouraged to see them as predators. This imagery continues throughout the play and forms an important part of its meaning.

Mosca informs Volpone that Voltore has brought him a present of a piece of plate engraved with his name and coat of arms. Volpone jokes that the plate should be engraved with a fox feigning death 'mocking a gaping crow'. Volpone sees himself as a fox misleading the predatory legacy hunters, thus continuing the comparison of people with animals. Some critics believe that bird and beast fables may have suggested the theme of *Volpone* to Jonson.

When Volpone asks why he is laughing, Mosca replies that it is because Voltore imagines that it is the last time he will have to bring a present for Volpone. If Volpone dies today leaving him everything, tomorrow he will be treated with the utmost respect. In a clear reference to Erasmus's *The Praise of Folly*, he says that if an ass wore the purple hood of the academic gown of a doctor of divinity, he would pass for a cathedral doctor. Mosca mocks both Voltore's greedy hopes and his stupidity. Volpone reveals his love of play-acting by the ease with which he adopts the role of invalid to deceive Voltore. He faithfully mimics the symptoms of several diseases, and mentions that he has thus misled the legacy hunters for three years, and as Voltore enters he gives a fake groan.

Act I, Scene iii

Summary

Mosca comes in with Voltore who is carrying the piece of plate, and he assures him that he is Volpone's favourite. He informs his master that Voltore has come to visit him, and has brought him a present. Volpone thanks him, tells him to come more often, and asks Mosca to bring him close so that he can feel his hand. Voltore declares that he is sorry to see Volpone so weak, and hypocritically adds that he wishes he could give him back his health. Mosca imparts the information that Volpone has made him his heir, whereupon Volpone pretends to be dying. In anticipation of his death, Mosca begs Voltore to take him into his household. Voltore assures him of his patronage, and Mosca goes on to tell Voltore that he already acts as his steward in taking care of Volpone's valuables, indicating that Voltore is to inherit everything. Voltore asks whether he is the only heir, and Mosca replies that he is, and that only this morning Volpone named him so in his will. Speaking with irony, Mosca says that his patron admires lawyers, and delivers a long speech explaining why he holds them in such high regard. This speech, which is ostensibly in praise of them, is in fact a bitter attack on members of the legal profession.

Their conversation is interrupted by knocking, and Mosca advises Voltore to leave unseen, while promising to bring him a copy of the inventory and the will. With the exit of Voltore, there is a short exchange between Volpone and Mosca, in which Mosca accepts Volpone's congratulations, before he announces the arrival of Corbaccio.

Commentary

This scene shows exactly how the magnifico extorts presents from his victims. In a form of confidence trick, Volpone plays on Voltore's greed to persuade him to make gifts to him, in the expectation of becoming his heir. Throughout the scene, Mosca's remarks and asides point out the true feelings of both Volpone and Voltore, beneath their hypocritical statements to each other. When Volpone asks to feel Voltore's hand, Mosca replies 'The plate is here sir', and when Voltore pretends to be sorry to see Volpone so weak, Mosca adds in an aside, that he is sorry 'That he is not weaker'. Jonson's satirical and ironical approach to his characters is particularly in evidence in this scene as he exposes their hypocrisy, and the audience cannot fail to be amused by the contrast between what they say and their real feelings.

Volpone's and Mosca's assessment of the avarice of the legacy hunters is accurate, and they manipulate and exploit this greed ruthlessly. Jonson's presentation of both Volpone and Voltore makes it quite clear to the audience that they are not only unscrupulous and greedy, but hypocritical as well. The view of human nature which is implied in this scene, is of man totally devoid of moral principles and dedicated only to financial profit. This pessimistic viewpoint is present throughout the play, but far from depressing the audience, Jonson moves it to laughter.

Jonson was influenced by the comedies of Aristophanes and by the theory, and practice, of ancient Greek writers of what is called Old Comedy, which flourished in Athens in the fourth century BC. Jonson had copies of Aristophanes' plays in his own library, and his work is full of borrowings from the Greek playwright. Some recent critics have drawn attention to their similarities. Aliki Dick has this to say of Jonson and Aristophanes: 'Yet, what Jonson shares with Aristophanes is his ardent zeal to censor social abuses and through laughter to ask man to become more reasonable.' Another feature which she has pointed out is that the plays of Aristophanes present two kinds of characters which were taken up by Jonson: the 'eirons' and the 'alazons'. The most appropriate translation of these terms is that of 'knaves' and 'gulls'. The eirons, or knaves, pretend to be less intelligent than they are, and both expose and use the weaknesses of the alazons, or gulls. In this scene Volpone shows himself to be a knave. He pretends to be sick and dying in order to expose and exploit the greed of Voltore, who is a gull, and encourage him to give him presents. Volpone deals in a similar fashion with all the legacy hunters.

But there is an additional perspective which can increase our understanding of Volpone's character and Jonson's dramatic purpose in his method of presenting Volpone. Building on Aliki Dick's discovery that Volpone is an eiron we can come to a deeper appreciation of Jonson's dramatic method. Let us briefly consider the etymology of the world 'irony'. The word comes from εἴρων (eiron) which was originally used in Greek Old Comedy for a man who is a dissembler, who pretends to know less than he does, and whose pronouncements often mean the opposite of what they seem. Our modern use and concept of irony have their basis in this. Volpone is, literally, an ironical man and many of his statements in the play are ironical in the true sense of the word. In his comments on the virtues of lawyers, as reported by Mosca, he seems to praise them while in fact he is making a savage criticism of them. His intended meaning is the exact opposite of the surface meaning:

> MOSCA   I oft have heard him say how he admired
> Men of your large profession, that could speak
> To every cause, and things mere contraries,
> Till they were hoarse again, yet all be law; (52–5)

Jonson's use of irony goes back to its origins. The more closely one examines Jonson's work, the more respect one has for the depth of his knowledge of ancient Greek drama, and the artistic uses to which he puts it.

The scene ends with a reiteration of the imagery of predatory birds, which is repeatedly associated with the legacy hunters, as Mosca announces the arrival of Corbaccio, and Volpone comments:

> The vulture's gone, and the old raven's come. (81)

Act I, Scene iv

Summary

Mosca tells Volpone to be silent and to feign sleep, and orders the piece of plate to multiply. He informs the audience that, although Corbaccio is weaker than Volpone could ever pretend to be, he hopes to jump over his grave. When Corbaccio enters Mosca welcomes him. Corbaccio enquires after Volpone's health, but he is hard of hearing and mishears Mosca's reply, so that he becomes alarmed when he thinks that he is getting better. But when Mosca reassures him that his health is in fact worse he is pleased. Corbaccio is quite shameless about his wish that Volpone should die. He enquires whether Volpone sleeps well, and on being told that he has not slept at all for two days, says that he should take some doctor's advice. He tells Mosca that he has a sleeping-draught from his own doctor. On being told that Volpone will not hear of any drug, he assures Mosca that he stood by while the draught was prepared, and saw all the ingredients, and that it will only make Volpone sleep. Mosca realises that it is poison and tells Corbaccio that not only does his master not believe in medicine, but also that he considers doctors to be more dangerous than disease.

Mosca now launches a sustained attack on doctors, which is not as vitriolic as the earlier one on lawyers and, in contrast to the previous one, is directly stated rather than ironically implied. He concludes with the statement that Volpone has said that no doctor should ever be his heir. Comically, Corbaccio mishears this and believes that Volpone has said that he would never be his heir. Mosca reassures him and continues his criticism of doctors in which Corbaccio joins. The conversation returns to the state of Volpone's health, and Corbaccio is jubilant when Mosca describes the seriousness of his physical condition, and how near death he is. He is now firmly convinced that he will outlive him.

Corbaccio asks whether Volpone has made his will and what he has left him. Mosca replies that the will has not been made and Corbaccio asks what Voltore was doing there. Mosca replies that he was drawn there when he heard that Volpone was making his will, which Mosca had urged him to do for Corbaccio's benefit. He also tells Corbaccio that Voltore had brought a present of a piece of plate. Suspicious as ever, Corbaccio enquires whether he has done this so that he will be named heir. Anxious that Voltore shall not forestall him, Corbaccio mentions that he has brought Volpone a present of a bag of gold coins, much heavier than Voltore's piece of plate. Mosca says that this is true medicine, and Corbaccio retorts that it is gold he can touch, even if he cannot drink it. Mosca suggests that they put it in his feeding-bowl, and goes on to say that it will cure him. Hearing this, Corbaccio is alarmed and wants to take his gold back (the last thing he wants is for Volpone to be cured).

Mosca tells him not to make such a mistake, but that he will advise him so that he will inherit all of Volpone's wealth. Corbaccio enquires how, and Mosca replies than when his patron has recovered and regained his senses he will ask him again to make his testament, and will show him Corbaccio's gift of the gold coins. Mosca also advises Corbaccio to go home quickly and to make his own will, leaving everything to Volpone. Corbaccio is surprised at this advice and asks whether he should disinherit his own son. Mosca says that this is only to make it appear more convincing. He asks Corbaccio to send him the will, and adds that when he comes to talk to Volpone, he will insist on Corbaccio's concern for him, his prayers, his many gifts, the present of gold coins, and finally – when he produces Corbaccio's will, which disinherits his own son in favour of Volpone – Volpone cannot fail, in return, to make out his will in Corbaccio's favour.

Corbaccio leaves and Volpone praises Mosca for his skill in tricking him. Then Volpone makes a speech in which he describes the cares and sickness attendant on old age. He goes on to mock Corbaccio for wanting to live longer, when he suffers from gout and palsy, and for hoping to restore his youth with magic charms. There is a knock on the door. It is the third of the suitors, Corvino. Volpone immediately lies down and resumes his pretence of being ill.

Commentary

One of the most extraordinary aspects of the play is the way that both Volpone and Mosca talk to gold and silver objects as if they were human. This is the other side of the reification effect in the play, in which people are treated as objects to be bought and sold; this applies to Celia in particular. At the beginning of the scene, Mosca urges the piece of plate to 'multiply', which would have shocked a Jacobean audience with its blasphemous reference to God's command to Adam and Eve to 'Be fruitful and multiply'. The effect is both amusing and sinister, for it indicates how completely Volpone and Mosca have reversed normal Christian values.

Corbaccio is another one of the gulls who are manipulated by Volpone. Corbaccio is so depraved that he does not even pretend to be concerned for Volpone's health, but unashamedly reveals his own self-interest:

> CORBACCIO   How does your patron?
> MOSCA   Truth, as he did, sir, no amends.
> CORBACCIO   What? mends he?
> MOSCA   No, sir, – he is rather worse.
> CORBACCIO   That's well. Where is he? (6–9)

Volpone's pretence of being ill not only profits him, but also exposes the naked greed of the fortune hunters. In this case, Corbaccio shows not only that he wishes Volpone dead, but that he is prepared to poison him in order to obtain his fortune, proving himself to be the most repellent and dangerous of the legacy hunters. He is also the oldest and feeblest. Much of the humour of this scene arises from the fact that Corbaccio is hard of hearing. Jonson skilfully uses this device to show Corbaccio's true feelings about Volpone, beneath the surface hypocrisy.

Jonson's satirical attack on doctors almost matches the vehemence of his earlier attack on lawyers. Seemingly he had scant respect for these visible members of the emerging middle class. But Jonson was by no means the first English writer to extract biting humour from these two occupations; Chaucer before him had made jokes at the expense of both doctors and lawyers.

Another of Corbaccio's vices is the delight that he takes in the supposed symptoms of Volpone's illness.

> MOSCA His mouth
> Is ever gaping, and his eyelids hang.
> CORBACCIO Good.
> MOSCA A freezing numbness stiffens all his joints,
> And makes the colour of his flesh like lead.
> CORBACCIO 'Tis good.
> MOSCA His pulse beats slow, and dull.
> CORBACCIO Good symptoms still. (42–5)

Eventually Corbaccio reveals that it is his desire to outlive Volpone that makes him take such an interest in his physical condition. The pleasure that he derives from another's pain makes him appear even more repulsive to the audience. Old age has not brought him wisdom or sympathy with another's suffering – quite the contrary. Like Voltore, Corbaccio openly indicates his interest in Volpone's will. Mosca craftily plays off Corbaccio and Voltore against each other by telling Corbaccio that Voltore has brought Volpone a piece of plate. Corbaccio is forced both to emulate, and to outdo this gift, with his present of a bag of gold coins. Mosca also gets him to disinherit his own son, Bonario, and to make out his will in Volpone's favour. Corbaccio loses all common sense and natural paternal feeling when in the grip of his greed, which Mosca both reveals and ruthlessly exploits.

The delight that Volpone takes in duping Corbaccio shows one of the strands in his own character, for not only does he manage to expose the greed of the would-be heirs and use it for his own ends, but he also takes a positive delight in outwitting them. Some critics have considered Volpone to be childish in this, but in fact, like Aristophanes before him, Jonson is using the eiron--alazon, the knave–gull relationship, in order to make a moral comment on how ridiculous human beings become when they fall prey to base impulses. Volpone is the agent by which the greed in Corbaccio's nature is revealed and punished and, like Aristophanes, Jonson has created a topsy-turvy world where all normal values are inverted, and for the first part of the play the evil are triumphant.

Act I, Scene v

Summary
Mosca greets Corvino obsequiously and informs him that Volpone is near death and recognises no one. Corvino asks Mosca's advice as to what he should do, for he has brought a pearl as a present.

Mosca replies that Volpone perhaps has enough memory left to know him, then he lies to Corvino, telling him that he is always calling his name, and on a more practical note, asks him if the pearl is from the East. Corvino answers that there has never been one equal to it in Venice. On hearing this, Volpone comes to life and calls his name faintly. Mosca tells him to present the pearl. Corvino asks him how he is feeling, and tells Mosca to let Volpone know that it is twenty-four carats in weight; he adds that he also has a diamond. Mosca says that it would be best if he showed the pearl.

When Corvino places the pearl in Volpone's hand, Volpone grasps it greedily. Corvino feigns concern at his condition and Mosca replies that he should ignore it and be cheerful. When Corvino questions him as to whether he is the heir Mosca replies that he has sworn not to show the will until Volpone is dead. He mentions that Corbaccio, Voltore and others have been there seeking legacies. But he says that he had taken advantage of the fact that Volpone was always calling 'Signior Corvino', had taken paper and ink, and asked him whom he would have as his heir. Volpone had replied: 'Corvino'. He had sent the other suitors home empty-handed, with nothing to do but to cry and to curse.

Mosca and Corvino embrace and Corvino asks whether Volpone can see. Mosca replies that he is blind, and tells him that he cannot recognise anyone and cannot remember anything. He cannot even remember the children whom he has fathered or brought up. The mention of children makes Corvino anxious, but Mosca replies that they are illegitimate, and it is rumoured that the dwarf, the hermaphrodite and the eunuch are all his. Corvino is reassured, but still asks whether Volpone can hear them. Mosca takes this opportunity to insult Volpone to his face, knowing full well that he cannot answer back, but must continue his pretence of being sick and senile. He curses Volpone, calling on the pox and plague to visit him, and goes on to insult his physical appearance. Corvino joins in with insults, now completely convinced that he is deaf.

Finally, Mosca asks Corvino to let him smother Volpone with a pillow. Corvino tells him to do as he wants, but he will leave. This indicates that he wants Mosca to kill Volpone but that he does not want to witness the actual murder. Before leaving, he wonders if he should take his pearl with him, but Mosca pours scorn on this suggestion, and also the idea that he should take his diamond. He assures Corvino that everything in the house belongs to him, and in order to get rid of him, mentions Celia, his wife. Corvino, who is a jealous husband, immediately leaves.

Instead of reproving Mosca for his insults and his growing independence of action, Volpone congratulates him. He tells his parasite that he wants to celebrate, and delights in the presents that he has received that morning. Mosca announces that Lady Would-Be is enquiring after his health, but Volpone tells him that he will only see her in three hours' time. Volpone mocks at the freedom the English allow their wives, and his assistant tells him that Sir Politic is as crafty as his name, for his wife is so ugly that no one will touch her, but if she had the face of Signior Corvino's wife, . . . he lets his voice trail away. His master is intrigued and he asks if she is beautiful. Mosca describes her and compares her to his gold. This catches Volpone's interest; he asks why he has not been told this before, and wants to see her. The parasite replies that she is guarded as carefully as his gold. This only serves to increase Volpone's desire to see her, and he determines to do so, even if only at her window. Mosca suggests that he adopt some disguise, and his master agrees.

Commentary

Corvino is the third of the legacy hunters to appear. Like the other victims he eagerly awaits the patrician's death, and is equally shameless about it. 'He is not dead?', he enquires when Mosca raises his hopes. Throughout this scene with Corvino, as with the other gulls Voltore and Corbaccio before him, Mosca manipulates and exploits his greed in a skilful fashion. The device of Volpone's pretended sickness is brilliantly used by Jonson, and in this particular scene he reveals not only the avarice of Corvino, but that of Volpone himself when Mosca urges Corvino to place the pearl he has brought into Volpone's hand:

> MOSCA   Put it into his hand; 'tis only there
> He apprehends – he has his feeling yet.
> See, how he grasps it! (17–19)

This physical representation of Volpone's grasping nature is sure to move the audience to laughter, particularly as he is supposed to be near death. Here, as in many places, in the play, Jonson demonstrates his mastery of irony.

The knave–gull relationship continues, with Mosca leading Corvino on by raising his hopes that he is heir. Prompted by his greed, Corvino gives Volpone not only the priceless pearl, but also a valuable diamond. Mosca strips away the pretences of the legacy hunters and reveals their naked greed, as when he tells Corvino not to feel sorry for his master:

> MOSCA   Tut, forget sir.
> The weeping of an heir should still be laughter
> Under a visor. (21–2)

'Visor' has the meaning of mask, and this short speech of Mosca's reveals the hypocrisy and pretence of all the would-be heirs. Instead of protesting against Mosca's statement, Corvino immediately picks

him up on the word 'heir': 'Why, am I his heir?' With consummate
ease Mosca dupes Corvino by telling him exactly what he wants to
hear – that he is indeed named as Volpone's heir.

Jonson's use of comedy in this scene even descends to the farcical,
and shows a skilful use of abusive language, one of the qualities for
which Aristophanes was famous. Mosca persuades Corvino that
Volpone is both deaf and blind and encourages him to insult him, and
in doing so forces him to reveal his true feelings about the man whose
heir he hopes to become.

But the scene also has sinister undertones: disease and sickness are
one of the major themes of the play, and Mosca suggests three things
that Venice was famous for, namely, the plague, licentious behaviour
and syphilis:

> MOSCA   The pox approach and add to your diseases,
> If it would send you hence the sooner, sir.
> For your incontinence, it hath deserved it
> Throughly, and throughly, and the plague to boot. (52–5)

Mosca's willingness and eagerness to insult his patron should warn
Volpone of his servant's underlying contempt for him, and his
growing independence. But the mood rapidly changes when Corvino
joins in the verbal abuse and shouts in Volpone's ear, as the series of
insults reaches a climax:

> CORVINO   His nose is like a common sewer, still running.
> MOSCA   'Tis good! And what his mouth?
> CORVINO   A very draught. (65–66)

The humour of the situation is increased for the audience by their
knowledge that Volpone can, in fact, hear everything that is being
said about him.

Mosca leads Corvino on still further, and even offers to smother his
master with his own pillow. Corvino shows himself to be as cold-
blooded as Corbaccio, who actually attempted to poison Volpone.
He wants Volpone dead, but he does not wish to be present when
Mosca kills him. The ease with which the parasite overcomes his
scruples is hilarious:

> CORVINO   I pray you, use no violence.
> MOSCA   No, sir? why?
> Why should you be thus scrupulous, pray you, sir?
> CORVINO   Nay, at your discretion (72–4)

Mosca's judgement of Corvino's character, and how to exploit his
weaknesses, extends to his perception that Corvino is a jealous

husband. In order to get him to leave, all Mosca has to do is to jokingly suggest sharing his wife.

When, at last, Volpone is alone with Mosca, he reveals another aspect of his character. He is addicted to the pleasures of the senses.

> VOLPONE   I will be troubled no more. Prepare
> Me music, dances, banquets, all delights;
> The Turk is not more sensual in his pleasures
> Than will Volpone (*Exit* MOSCA) Let me see, a pearl!
> A diamond! plate! chequeens! Good morning's purchase; (86–90)

However, his strongest emotion seems to be the pleasure of acquisition. Mosca shows his ability to play on the desires not only of the legacy hunters, but also his patron. When he notices Volpone's interest in the beauty of Corvino's wife, he excites and increases it with a hyperbolic description calculated to appeal to Volpone's instincts:

> VOLPONE   Has she so rare a face?
> MOSCA   O, sir, the wonder,
> The blazing star of Italy! a wench
> O' the first year! a beauty ripe as harvest
> Whose skin is whiter than a swan, all over!
> Than silver, snow, or lilies! a soft lip,
> Would tempt you to eternity of kissing!
> And flesh that melteth in the touch to blood!
> Bright as your gold! and lovely as your gold! (107–14)

The series of hyperboles and inflammatory comparisons, which are intended to excite Volpone sexually, culminate in a simile aimed directly at his strongest emotion: his lust for gold: 'Bright as your gold! and lovely as your gold!'

Mosca immediately captures Volpone's interest:

> VOLPONE   Why had I not known this before? (114)

Mosca artfully increases Volpone's desire to see her by telling him:

> O, not possible;
> She's kept as warily as is your gold . . . (116–117)

The difficulty of seeing her only serves to inflame Volpone further. Mosca indicates that he is able to manipulate not only the legacy hunters, but also his master. Whereas Volpone seems to have strong desires, even if unnatural ones, Mosca appears to be without desires of any kind, apart from the one to better himself. Mosca shows clearly that he has the upper hand in his relationship with Volpone, and later in the play he attempts to outwit even him.

Act II, Scene i

Summary
The action moves out of Volpone's house to a square nearby where Corvino lives. An English traveller, Sir Politic Would-Be, is trying to impress the younger Peregrine with his knowledge and experience of foreign parts, but succeeds in conveying the opposite to what he means, and shows himself to be naive in the extreme. He tells Peregrine that he has come to Venice because of his wife's desire for sightseeing and her wish to learn the language. When Peregrine mentions that it is only seven weeks since he left England, Sir Politic asks him for news. But it appears from his questions that the knight is only interested in the trivial and the bizarre, and is highly superstitious to boot. He enquires whether, as he has heard, a raven has built its nest in a ship belonging to the king. In an aside Peregrine wonders whether Sir Politic is trying to make a fool of him, or whether he is making a fool of himself, and asks who he is. Sir Politic Would-Be gives his name, and in another aside Peregrine says that his name reveals his character. It also transpires that Peregrine has heard of Sir Politic, and asks him if it is his wife, the fine Lady Would-Be, who is staying in Venice to study fashion and behaviour among the Venetian courtesans. Peregrine leads the foolish knight on by playing on his interest in superstitious omens, and concludes by giving a ridiculous account of a whale which he says reached Woolwich, and has waited for months in order to subvert the Stode fleet. Sir Politic seizes on this and insists that the whale was sent by Spain or Austria (enemies of England at the time).

Peregrine also informs Sir Politic that Stone the jester is dead. When he hears this, Sir Politic declares that Stone was a dangerous spy, who received weekly from the Low Countries intelligence concealed in cabbages, and sent it hidden inside fruit, and even oysters, to ambassadors. Peregrine is astounded at this, but Sir Politic assures him that he has observed him at a public eating-house receiving information in a trencher of meat from a secret agent disguised as a traveller, and immediately sending out answers hidden in a toothpick. When Peregrine queries this Sir Politic states that the meat was cut and laid out in the form of a secret code. Peregrine retorts that he has heard that the jester could not read. To this Sir Politic's reply is that this was cunningly given out by his employers to fool people. He asserts that Stone could not only read, but was a master of foreign languages and highly intelligent. Peregrine interrupts to lead him on further, by telling him that he has heard that

baboons are spies. This provokes a further outburst of nonsense from
Sir Politic's fevered brain.

Throughout the scene Sir Politic has been pretending to be
extremely knowledgeable, and he now informs Peregrine that he has
a good knowledge of affairs of state which he observes for his private
advantage. Continuing to deceive him, Peregrine says that he considers himself lucky to have met him, for his knowledge will help to
instruct him how to behave, as he is still young and ignorant. Sir
Politic asks him whether he has travelled abroad without any
knowledge or advice. Peregrine tells him that he had some rules from
a grammar book, which his Italian teacher taught him. But his
would-be new adviser scorns these and informs Peregrine that he has
often been consulted by noble persons concerning their sons. His
speech is interrupted by Peregrine who draws his attention to the
approach of some people.

Commentary
Act II introduces us to the sub-plot which concerns the relationship
between Sir Politic Would-Be and Peregrine. The sub-plot echoes the
main plot in several respects and also provides an oblique commentary on it. As in the main plot, a foolish character who believes himself
crafty is outwitted by an ironical character who leads him on and
tricks him. Sir Politic Would-Be who, as his name suggests, likes to
think of himself as worldly-wise and cunning, plays the gull to
Peregrine, who leads him on to make a fool of himself, and can
therefore be considered a knave. Unlike the situation in the main
plot, the eiron–alazon or knave–gull relationship is ultimately for Sir
Politic's good and leads to his achieving deeper self-knowledge,
whereas, in the main plot, the machinations of Volpone work to the
detriment of his victims, and are primarily aimed at fraudulently
extracting money and other favours from them.

Another function of the sub-plot is to provide light relief from the
more serious main plot. This is evident from the very first appearance
of Sir Politic in the square in front of Corvino's house. In his attempt
to impress Peregrine with his knowledge and experience as a traveller, Sir Politic conveys the opposite impression from his very first
words in the play:

> Sir, to a wise man, all the world's his soil. (1)

He begins his speech with a commonplace about the wise man being
at home anywhere. Unfortunately he inadvertently makes an outrageous pun on 'soil' which as well as meaning 'native land', as he
intends, could also mean 'filth' or even 'sewage' in Jonson's time. The
result is that instead of appearing to be a worldly-wise character, he
appears a complete fool.

Jonson's linguistic inventiveness is shown in this use of the pun. The pun operates in a similar way to metaphor, linking two quite different areas of human experience in a single figure of speech. It involves a play on the meanings of words where the surface meaning is subverted by the hidden meaning. In this instance an apothegm, or wise saying, about travel is subverted by the double meaning of 'soil' which could also mean faecal matter. Sir Politic's airy pretence of being at home anywhere in Europe is totally undermined and the audience laughs at his stupidity. In the first line of his speech Jonson contrasts Sir Politic's pretentiousness with the absurd reality. The pun, therefore, has contributed to the characterisation of Sir Politic.

The speech continues with Sir Politic's lengthy and pompous justification of, and reasons for, travelling. He says that it is no wanton desire to see foreign countries that makes him travel or a wish to change his religion, nor is he disloyal to the country where he was born. He is not a traveller for the old-fashioned notion of getting to know different minds and manners like Ulysses:

> much less
> That idle, antique, stale, grey-haired project
> Of knowing men's minds and manner, with Ulysses;
> But a peculiar humour of my wife's, (8–11)

Sir Politic's lofty comparison of himself with Homer's heroic character in *The Odyssey*, who was famous both for his cunning and for the many years of travel which he took to return home from the Fall of Troy to Ithaca and his wife Penelope, serves only to make him appear even more ridiculous. There is, however, an extreme appropriateness in the reference to Ulysses, because Sir Politic's reason for travel is also his wife. The humorous contrast between the heroic and cunning Ulysses returning from the sack of Troy, and the pretentious, foolish and cowardly Sir Politic, who has travelled to Venice on a whim of his wife, adds to the comedy of the speech, and demonstrates again with what devastating accuracy Jonson used his knowledge of classical literature.

Sir Politic's speech ends with another amusing pun:

> I hope you travel, sir, with licence? (14)

In the days when Jonson was writing Englishmen needed official permission – a licence – to travel abroad. However, 'licence' had another meaning, which it still carries today, of 'licentiousness' or 'excessive liberty' and 'disregard for law and propriety', which totally undermines the seriousness of what he is saying.

His very first speech, therefore, reveals both his pretentiousness and foolishness. Jonson contrives this brilliantly through his use of such resources as the pun, and the contrast between the pompous and elevated tone of Sir Politic's speech and the absurd and comic reality. By playing between these two levels Jonson creates his comic effects, and indicates how the audience is to perceive the function of the character of Sir Politic Would-Be, which is to provide comic relief from the main plot.

The names of the dramatis personae in Jonson's plays often give clues to the audience about their characters. Sir Politic Would-Be suggests a man who wants the world to think that he is cunning and worldly-wise. 'Peregrine' as well as meaning 'falcon' could also mean 'traveller' or 'pilgrim'. The falcon is in obvious contrast to the parrot 'Sir Pol' and Peregrine, in contrast to Sir Politic, stands for normality and good judgement, and shows up the other's pretentious absurdity. Peregrine is one of a long line of gentleman wits who appear in Jonson's comedies and represent normality. Jonson's attitude towards the character of Peregrine is entirely uncritical, unlike his attitude towards most of the characters in the play. The developing relationship, in which Peregrine leads Sir Politic on to expose his foolishness, is the main concern of the sub-plot.

When Peregrine first hears Sir Politic's foolish enquiry about the raven's nest, he wonders if Sir Politic is trying to make a fool of him, but as soon as he learns his name, he realises that he is a foolish person trying to pass himself off as a wise one. (Jonson frequently uses the aside as a dramatic device to reveal the true thoughts of one character about another.) Once Peregrine realises to whom he is speaking, he sets out to lead him on. The motive behind his mention of superstitious omens, is to expose Sir Politic's gullibility, which is in extreme contrast to his pose of a knowledgeable traveller.

When Sir Politic asks for more news and Peregrine tells him that Stone the jester is dead, Sir Politic makes another of his excruciating and unintentional puns, which were no doubt enjoyed by Jonson's original audience, but which need some explaining for a modern one. Two meanings can be disentangled from 'Mas' Stone': 'Master Stone', the name of the jester and 'Marston', the name of one of Jonson's fellow playwrights whose literary style Jonson had mocked in *The Poetaster*. But Jonson does not let it conclude here. He squeezes the last drop of humour from the pun by having Sir Politic say 'Stone dead', meaning both that the jester Stone is dead and that he is 'stone' dead, meaning absolutely dead. Jonson is fond of verbal jokes and *Volpone* is full of such word-play.

Jonson is also highly ironical and praises himself when he has Peregrine say of Sir Politic in an aside:

O this knight
(Were he well known) would be a precious thing
To fit our English stage. He that should write
But such a fellow, should be thought to feign
Extremely if not maliciously. (55–60)

Peregrine mercilessly exposes Sir Politic's gullibility and lays the ground for future tricks he will play on him, by claiming to be ignorant of travel and in need of help from Sir Politic, which of course Sir Politic is only too happy to volunteer.

Act II, Scene ii

Summary

As Sir Politic and Peregrine stand talking in the square, Mosca and Nano approach, disguised as mountebank's assistants, and begin to erect a stage. Sir Politic begins an argument about mountebanks with Peregrine, who says that they are quacks; Sir Politic, on the other hand, maintains that they are the most learned men in Europe and excellent doctors.

Volpone enters, disguised as the mountebank Scoto of Mantua, climbs onto the stage, and proceeds to make his sales pitch. He compares himself favourably with the other mountebanks, whom he dismisses, and he also pours scorn on the charlatans. Sir Politic Would-Be is struck by the speech and praises it to Peregrine. Volpone begins a discourse on the virtues of health and praises his ointment. He points out that gold cannot cure sickness by contact alone; only his oil has that power. He gives a comprehensive list of illnesses that he claims his medicine will cure. One of his assistants, Nano, sings a song praising the oil above the discoveries of Hippocrates and Galen, two famous physicians of Ancient Greece. Volpone continues extravagantly to praise the healing powers of his oil, and also emphasises the amount of work he put into its discovery. He pretends to reduce its price from eight to six crowns. Finally, he asks his audience to throw their handkerchiefs to him with the money tied inside. Celia, from her window, throws her handkerchief, and Volpone acknowledges it, saying that as well as the oil he will give her a powder which has the capacity to restore youth.

Commentary

At the time that Jonson was writing, mountebanks were one of the famous sights of Venice, and there is a long description of them in a contemporary travel book, *Coryate's Crudities*. It is appropriate that Volpone should disguise himself as one, and natural that Sir Politic and Peregrine should be curious about them. Sir Politic shows his gullibility when he says of them: 'They are the most knowing men of Europe! Great scholars, excellent physicians.'

With Volpone's entrance, in the disguise of the mountebank Scoto of Mantua, Jonson shows his mastery of the kind of medical jargon used by such hucksters. Volpone's speeches clearly fall into the domain of rhetoric, which can be defined as discourse which attempts to persuade. Volpone, as Scoto, intends both to impress his listeners in his favour and to persuade them to buy his wares. Jonson's writing reveals a thorough knowledge of rhetoric, which is one of the subjects he would have studied at Westminster School, and also in his reading of Cicero and Quintilian, both of whom he admired.

Volpone employs specific rhetorical devices in his sales speeches. In the first instance he applies the mode of persuasion known as ethical appeal. He tries to ingratiate himself with his audience by creating the impression that he is a man of honesty. He does this in the first place by praising himself, then by dismissing rumours about his supposed poisoning of Cardinal Bembo's cook. Thirdly, and most amusingly, he launches a bitter attack on the charlatans, his rivals, in a speech which is remarkable for its inspired abuse:

> Those turdy-facy-nasty-paty-lousy-fartical rogues . . . (61)

This use of derogatory compound adjectives is reminiscent of Aristophanes, who was famous for his inspired use of abusive language. Jonson's own linguistic virtuosity and talent for verbal abuse is clearly demonstrated in the speech. Even Sir Politic is struck by it, and asks Peregrine: 'Ha' you heard better language sir?' Yet again, Sir Politic shows how easily he is impressed, this time by the huckster's excoriation. The technique of criticising your business competitors is used in advertising even today.

Volpone's use of rhetoric veers to that of the emotional appeal, a device well known in classical oratory, in which the speaker attempts to play on the audience's emotions. In this case Volpone tries to appeal to their fear of sickness and wish for health in a rhetorical question: 'O, health! health! the blessing of the rich! the riches of the Poor! who can buy thee at too dear a rate, since there is no enjoying the world without thee?' The aim of rhetoric is to persuade, and this Volpone does supremely well. It should be remembered that in Jonson's comedies jargon and rhetoric are only used by the most reprehensible characters. Jonson was apparently suspicious of the ability to sway people in this way.

Throughout the play a connection is established between health and riches, both in the action and in the language. Volpone attempts to motivate his audience to open their purses by playing on their fear of sudden death: 'Be not so sparing of your purses, honourable gentlemen, as to abridge the natural course of life'. Having frightened his audience, Volpone tells them that gold cannot cure sickness by touch alone, only his ointment has that power. He now launches into a speech describing all the diseases that his patent medicine will cure. This is full of the medical jargon of the time and, in order further to impress his audience with his learning, Volpone includes many Latin names for the various illnesses. Jonson reveals a knowledge of the medical terminology of his time just as in his play *The Alchemist* he deftly uses the technical terms of alchemy.

In this scene Volpone's speeches show a skilful use of the art of persuasion and a knowledge of the best way to part people from their money. He praises the healing powers of his oil, and also exaggerates the amount of work he put into its discovery, a method still used in advertising. Finally in a sales technique which, similarly, is employed even today by market traders, he pretends to reduce its price from eight to six crowns. The whole purpose of Volpone's disguise as a mountebank, and the underlying motive of all his speeches, is to catch sight of Celia. She now appears at the window and throws down her handkerchief containing money to buy the patent medicine. Volpone has achieved his purpose and, to attract her interest still further, promises to give her a powder which bestows eternal youth.

Act II, Scene iii

Summary
Volpone's speech to Celia is interrupted by the entrance of Corvino, her husband, who is jealous, and beats away Volpone and his assistants. Sir Politic Would-Be foolishly believes that the attack is somehow directed at him for political motives, and announces that he will go home. Peregrine encourages him in his mistake and he leaves.

Commentary
This short scene makes Corvino's jealousy abundantly plain to the audience. He refers to the situation in terms of the 'commedia dell'arte', casting himself as Pantalone di Besogniosi, who was the elderly cuckold in such entertainments. The 'commedia dell'arte' was an improvised drama, relying on stock situations, which was popular in Italy in the sixteenth century, and Jonson shows his knowledge of Italy and Venice in using such references. The dramatist's intention in this is to foreshadow ironically Corvino's later willingness to prostitute his wife to Volpone. By casting himself in the foolish and conventional rôle of the jealous and cuckolded husband, Corvino makes his later acquiescence in offering his own wife to another man even more funny. Further dramatic irony is added by the fact that Corvino is jealous of Volpone in his disguise of Scoto, and it is to Volpone that he offers his wife later in the play. The conversation between Sir Politic and Peregrine is also relevant to later developments in the play. Sir Politic reveals his paranoia and fear of plots against himself, in which belief Peregrine encourages him, so that he can use it against him when the opportunity arises. Although this is an extremely short scene it is crucially important to the development of both the main plot and the sub-plot.

Act II, Scene iv

Summary
Volpone and Mosca appear again in the square and Volpone
announces that he has fallen in love with Celia. Mosca expresses the
wish that Volpone had never seen her and Volpone for his part says
that it would have been better if Mosca had not told him about her.
The parasite promises to do his best to relieve Volpone's torment,
and in return his patron places all his wealth at Mosca's disposal for
this purpose. Mosca urges his master to be patient and assures him
that he will satisfy his desire for Celia. Volpone wonders if his
disguise as Scoto was convincing, and Mosca assures him that it was.

Commentary
Volpone dramatises his love for Celia in a parody of the Elizabethan
love sonnet. Jonson's audience would have been familiar with the
metaphor of being wounded by Cupid which was used by Sir Philip
Sidney, in imitation of the Petrarchan sonnet, in his *Astrophel and
Stella* sequence which appeared in 1591. Volpone begins the scene
with the conventional lover's complaint: 'O, I am wounded.' This is
ironically undercut by Mosca's immediate question: 'Where, sir?'
Then, in an amusing travesty of the love sonnet, Volpone declares his
love for Celia:

> But angry Cupid, bolting from her eyes,
> Hath shot himself into me like a flame,
> Where now he flings about his burning heat,
> As in a furnace an ambitious fire
> Whose vent is stopped. (3–7)

The references to Cupid shooting forth the flames of love from
Celia's eyes begins an extended metaphor using conventional imagery of love as fire, but which rapidly descends to the realism of the
word 'furnace'. The effect of this is added to, with the prosaic detail
that the 'vent is stopped'. The sudden decline from the elevated
diction of the Petrarchan love sonnet to the absurdly realistic
language used in the comparison of the heat of his love to a stopped
furnace, would have induced laughter in his audience, and Jonson's
intention is clearly humorous. The comparison continues with Volpone's absurd reference to his liver, a part of the human anatomy never
mentioned in the Elizabethan love sonnet.

> My liver melts, and I, without the hope
> Of some soft air from her refreshing breath,
> Am but a heap of cinders. (9–11)

The final, ridiculous image of himself, as a 'heap of cinders', suggests that the fires of love have consumed him, but the use of the exact, homely, and realistic word 'cinders' reduces the whole speech to absurdity.

This outburst by the aged lecher, in which he describes himself burning with lust like a furnace, is both ridiculous and funny to the audience. It seems that even Volpone has fallen prey to desire, and it is this weakness, and the loss of control which it entails, which causes him to expose himself to danger. Despite the high-flown phrases with which Volpone begins his declaration of love, by the end of it the audience is left in no doubt that his feelings towards Celia are pure lust. Through his knowledge of the poetic conventions of his time, Jonson manages to subvert the sentiments of the Elizabethan love sonnet, by his careful choice of poetic diction, in which he places prosaic and realistic words in juxtaposition with idealistic and elevated language and imagery, thus producing an effect of incongruity and, ultimately, hilarious comedy.

Our sense of the absurdity of Volpone's professed love for Celia increases when he asks Mosca to help him obtain the object of his desire:

> VOLPONE . . . Mosca, take my keys,
> Gold, plate, and jewels, all's at thy devotion;
> Employ them how thou wilt; nay, coin me, too,
> So thou, in this, but crown my longings. (21–4)

Volpone has revealed still more completely his debased notion of love when he offers Mosca that which he holds dearest, namely his wealth, if Mosca will help him. Volpone believes that anything can be bought, even love. In the imagery and metaphors he employs, Jonson has Volpone condemn himself out of his own mouth. This ends with his absurd invitation to Mosca to 'coin' him too, or make him into money. This is part of the reification effect of the play in which people are treated like objects to be bought and sold.

Act II, Scene v

Summary

The action moves to Corvino's house. Corvino reveals his jealousy in a long speech in which he berates Celia for looking out of the window at the mountebank, who he does not realise is Volpone in disguise. He is scathing about the supposed Scoto's appearance in an attempt to belittle him in Celia's eyes. He makes several cruel and unjustified sexual gibes at her expense, accusing her of wanting to have sex with the mountebank. Corvino also tells her that he will announce himself a cuckold and will keep her dowry and when she asks him to be patient he threatens her with his sword.

Celia, who is innocent of his accusations, wonders why her being at the window now should make him more angry than at other times. Corvino replies that giving Scoto her handkerchief was an attempt to arrange a meeting with him. Protesting her innocence, Celia says that the only time she leaves the house is to go to church, and even that is seldom. Corvino replies that she shall go out even less and threatens to have the window blocked up and to chalk a line two or three yards from it which she is not to cross. He will also force her to wear a chastity belt, and all her activity in future will be confined to the house. Corvino's ravings at his wife are interrupted by Mosca knocking at the door.

Commentary

Corvino's speech, is a remarkable portrayal of jealousy, which was considered to be one of the vices, like avarice, previously displayed in the first speech of the play. Jonson's implied ideal throughout the play is that of moderation and balance in human behaviour. Corvino's excessive jealousy and raving indicates that he has lost his self-control. The deeper irony of the scene lies in the fact that the fierce sexual jealousy he reveals is directed at Volpone in his disguise as the mountebank, and in the very next scene he will agree to prostitute his wife to Volpone.

The speech begins with Corvino referring to his honour, in an ironical foreshadowing of his later claim in III.vii that honour is unimportant. Jonson's careful construction of the play is apparent in such details. Jonson's talent for invective and abusive language provides splendid opportunities for the actors and also delights the audience:

> CORVINO   Death of mine honour, with the city's fool?
> A juggling, tooth-drawing, prating mountebank? (1–2)

Corvino almost spits out the words; the dental sounds in 'tooth', 'prating' and 'mountebank', all pronounced with the tongue against the teeth, give guidance to the actor both as to how they are to be delivered, and with what venom. Jonson's awareness of the subtleties and resources of dramatic language extends to the sounds and enunciation of words, an important factor if they are to be spoken on stage. He also took a great deal of care with the punctuation of his plays, so that the actors would give his words their intended meaning. All this attention to detail reveals him to be a consummate dramatic craftsman. The playwright's total mastery of dramatic dialogue is shown most clearly in extended speeches like this one, in which a protagonist reveals himself to the audience in virtuoso speeches, where Jonson's delight in the sounds and effects of spoken language is evident.

The note throughout the speech is one of contempt, and the picture drawn by Corvino of the disguised Volpone is the least flattering one possible. There is an insistence on his bedraggled and ruffianly appearance and his tawdry finery:

> Or were you enamoured of his copper rings?
> His saffron jewel, with the toad-stone in't?
> Or his embroidered suit, with the cope-stitch,
> Made of a hearse-cloth? or his old tilt-feather?
> Or his starched beard? (11–15)

Having delivered a scathing attack on Celia's supposed would-be paramour and disposed of him, Corvino turns his attention to her. His jealousy rises to heights of sexual hysteria:

> Well! you shall have him, yes.
> He shall come home, and minister unto you
> The fricace, for the mother. Or let me see,
> I think you'd rather mount? Would you not mount?
> Why, if you'll mount, you may; yes truly, you may;
> And so you may be seen, down to th'foot. (15–20)

The entire speech is full of bitter sexual innuendo directed by the insanely jealous Corvino at his wife. 'Have him' literally means to have sex with him. 'The fricace for the mother' suggests both massage and sexual intercourse (literally massage that will make a mother). To 'mount' is to assume the male and superior position in love-making. 'Foot' both in Jonson and in Shakespeare can mean copulation, from the French verb 'foutre'. Corvino also ironically invites her to 'make one' with the mountebank, or to join in sexual congress with him. The whole scene shows Corvino to be in the grip of the most savage sexual jealousy, and this is vividly conveyed by Jonson in the tone and the language.

Act II, Scene vi

Summary
Corvino hopes that Mosca has come to announce Volpone's death. But Mosca tells him that far from dying, Volpone has made an amazing recovery, due to Scoto's oil, which Corbaccio and Voltore have bought. Corvino's rage at the mountebank increases and he swears that he could kill him. He also doubts that the medicine would have the power to cure Volpone, as it is made of bizarre ingredients.

Mosca replies that they poured some in his ears and some in his nostrils and gave him a massage or 'fricace'. The mention of the world 'fricace' adds to Corvino's fury because it reminds him of what he himself said to his wife. Mosca goes on to say that in addition they have consulted the College of Physicians on how to restore Volpone's health. Here, Jonson launches an attack on doctors, mocking their absurd cures. After suggesting various outlandish remedies, Mosca says that the physicians have finally agreed that the only way to save Volpone is for a young woman to sleep with him.

The parasite claims that all the other legacy hunters are competing with each other as to who shall be the first to present Volpone with a young woman. He urges Corvino to forestall them if he can. (Of course this is a cunning ruse to get Corvino to offer Celia to Volpone.) Corvino suggests that it would be best to hire some common prostitute. Mosca's answer to this is to say that she could easily cheat them all out of Volpone's money, and he goes on to say that it must be some straightforward woman with no tricks, and asks Corvino if he does not have some kinswoman. He implores Corvino to think, and concludes by saying that one of the doctors has offered up his daughter for the task. Corvino is surprised at this and Mosca adds that she is also a virgin. He states categorically that the only thing that can restore Volpone is a young woman and, besides, only a few people will know.

Corvino manages to convince himself, and tells Mosca that he will offer his wife. Mosca's reply to this is that he would have suggested it himself at the beginning, only he did not want to seem to be advising it. Mosca now assures him that they have outwitted all the others, and when Volpone next has a fit they can let him die. They only have to pull the pillow away from under his head and he will choke to death. He volunteers the information that he would have done it before, but for Corvino's scruples. The merchant now asks Mosca to tell Volpone that he is willing to offer him his wife. Mosca's response is that the other legacy hunters will be banished and only Corvino will be received.

Commentary

Jonson realised the difficulties involved in rapid scene changes, a particular problem in the public theatres, because they did not have the benefit of extensive scenery and changes of location had to be mainly indicated in the dialogue of the play. The whole of the first act established the claustrophobic atmosphere of Volpone's household and took place entirely there. In the second act the action moves to the outside world of Venice, for the sub-plot, and for Volpone's impersonation of the mountebank. This leads naturally in scenes five six and seven into Corvino's house, where the oppressive nature of his sexual jealousy is shown, and we are again supposedly in an enclosed interior.

Scene six is carefully crafted by Jonson to reveal how easily the merchant Corvino is persuaded by Mosca to offer his wife to Volpone, through exploitation of his greed, and despite his jealous ravings. Jonson makes great use of dramatic irony. The audience knows that Scoto and Volpone are the same person but Corvino does not. His jealous outburst at Scoto, and the ease with which Mosca persuades him to offer his wife to the very person of whom he is so jealous continues the long running joke.

Another feature of the scene is Jonson's lengthy satirical attack on doctors, in the outlandish cures suggested by the College of physicians, as related by Mosca:

> MOSCA   Where one would have a cataplasm of spices,
> Another, a flayed ape clapped to his breast,
> A third would ha' it a dog, a fourth an oil
> With wild cats' skins . . .   (29–32)

What finally persuades Corvino to offer his wife is his fear that the doctor Signior Lupio will forestall him by offering Volpone his virgin daughter, and so inherit his fortune instead of him.

Act II, Scene vii

Summary

Corvino calls out for Celia and she comes in weeping. He tells her to dry her eyes and says that he is not jealous. He claims that he never was jealous. He knows that if women wish to be false to their husbands they will do so despite being guarded. He tells her to get ready straight away, to put on her best clothes and her finest jewels, because they are invited to a feast at old Volpone's house, where he will show her how far he is from being jealous.

Commentary

The short scene indicates how vacillating Corvino is and how easily he can be swayed by others, if motivated by greed. Celia is still in tears from the tongue-lashing he has given her because of his jealousy of Scoto, and now he tells her to dry her eyes. Celia rightly doubts his sudden change of mood, his protestation that he is not jealous, and his denial that he ever was. What he says next: 'And that the fiercest spies are tamed with gold?' is full of dramatic irony, because it is he himself who has been tamed with gold, and not even gold: only the promise of it. His sudden change of mood has been brought about by Mosca raising his hopes of becoming Volpone's heir if he offers his wife to him. Irony is piled on irony as he urges Celia to dress up and look her best. He is in fact acting as pander to his own wife in telling her to look her most beautiful, because he wants to procure her for Volpone. The final irony is in the last two lines of the scene, when he says:

> . . . where it shall appear
> How far I am from jealousy or fear. (17–18)

Act III, Scene i

Summary
The opening scene of the third act is entirely taken up with a long soliloquy from Mosca in which he praises his profession of parasite and displays his character to the audience. Mosca is extremely pleased with himself at this juncture, because it seems that his knavery is working out according to plan, and that he has managed to hoodwink all the legacy hunters.

Commentary
Just as his master has delivered a soliloquy in praise of gold, revealing that he suffers from one of the seven deadly sins – covetousness, now Mosca praises his dubious means of earning a living, that of parasite in Volpone's household, showing that the deadly sin that he exemplifies is that of pride. This paean of praise for parasitism is as unnatural as Volpone's speech in praise of gold. The word 'parasite' literally means one who eats at the table of another, at the other's expense. The unnatural values held by Mosca, in that he praises something that most people would be ashamed of, indicate the reversal of normal values in the two main characters of the play. It is Mosca's sheer brazenness which shocks the audience; there is no sense of guilt at doing evil, only pride in his own cleverness. It is quite apparent from the speech that Mosca is completely amoral, and would no doubt have been considered a Machiavellian by the original audience, because of his total lack of conscience and his delight and skill in plotting and scheming. It also becomes apparent that he is his own man and not just subservient to his master. This fact is important for the future development of the action.

Mosca's speech is full of imagery and comparisons more appropriate to describing the growth of plants: 'spring and burgeon'. It is of course possible for the actor taking the part of Mosca to play this speech in a *risqué* way, interpreting 'prosperous parts' as a sexual pun referring to his private parts. What is apparent in the speech is Mosca's self-love and his inordinate pride. Mosca compares the superior parasite, which he clearly considers himself to be, and who he says is 'dropped from above', with the 'clotpoles' who are bred on earth, and he goes on to wonder why the craft of parasitism was 'not made into a science'. Mosca's world view is extremely cynical and debased:

> Almost
> All the wise world is little else in nature
> But parasites, or sub-parasites. (11–13)

He is trying to justify his ignoble occupation to himself by presenting a nightmare vision of society, with people as predators preying on one another. Not only is Mosca entirely unself-critical, but he is puffed up with pride at his own cleverness. Mosca goes on to say, that he is not talking about parasites who only manage to get enough to eat, or those who are obsequious to their master. He is speaking about one who is mercurial and able to deal with all his master's moods, and all situations. Such a creature is born with the art, does not struggle to learn it, but practises it as a natural ability; such 'Are the true parasites'.

The idea that a servant should be more clever than his master has become almost a cliché or commonplace today. We have only to think of Figaro or Jeeves. However, Mosca's schemes are put to the service of evil, to enrich Volpone by means of a confidence trick which both exposes and exploits human greed. Eventually Mosca meets his downfall when he attempts to outwit his master. Mosca's fatal weakness is the overweening pride which he takes in his own villainy and his ability to outwit others. It is this which causes him to overreach himself and brings about his downfall.

The soliloquy gives Jonson the opportunity to develop and reveal Mosca's shameless character to the audience. Mosca's delight in tricking others deepens our sense of the unnaturalness of the world of *Volpone*, where normal human values are absent and the only emotions on display are greed, lust and avarice. The work is therefore reminiscent of the comedies of Aristophanes, in that only negative human qualities are foregrounded and in its belief that the world is made up of eirons and alazons.

Act III, Scene ii

Summary
After Mosca's speech of self-revelation, which he has made in the street, Bonario appears. Mosca greets him obsequiously, but it is plain that Bonario has no liking for Mosca and no wish to talk to him. Bonario also makes it obvious that he despises the way Mosca earns his living. In reply, Mosca claims that Bonario's accusations are

unfair because such charges are easily made, he is above him in station and, besides, he does not know him. Craftily Mosca pretends to cry. Bonario is easily deceived and regrets that he was so harsh to Mosca, who excuses his way of earning his livelihood by saying that he has no choice because he has no money. Cunningly he claims that he is innocent of the very things that he is in fact busily doing. Bonario is taken in, and begs Mosca to forgive him and to tell him what he wants. To further his deception Mosca reveals that Bonario's father is about to disinherit him, and says that although it has nothing to do with him, he is telling him about it from a disinterested concern for goodness and virtue, which he hears abound in Bonario. Bonario is shocked by Mosca's revelations and refuses to believe that his father could be so unnatural. The parasite promises to bring him to where he will hear himself being disinherited by his own father, and Bonario agrees to come with him.

Commentary
It is an essential part of Jonson's dramatic purpose that Mosca and Bonario meet in this scene. Having just revealed Mosca's depravity to the audience, he immediately contrasts it with Bonario's goodness, bringing together these polar opposites. 'Bonario' in Florio's Italian dictionary was defined as 'honest, good, uncorrupt'. When Bonario instantly shows his dislike of Mosca and his occupation, this follows so closely on Mosca's long speech in praise of himself and the profession of parasite, that it makes an implied comment on Mosca's speech, and suggests the standards of normality and decency by which Mosca must ultimately be judged.

Mosca's crafty pretence of friendship towards Bonario and his hypocritical show of distress at Bonario's accusations, effortlessly deceive him. In a speech of the greatest irony, Mosca claims to be innocent of the very activities he is in fact engaged in:

> But that I have done
> Base offices, in rending friends asunder,
> Dividing families, betraying counsels,
> Whispering false lies, or mining men with praises,
> Trained their credulity with perjuries,
> Corrupted chastity . . . (25–34)

This is the only time in the play that Mosca mentions his underhand activities to anyone but his master, but ironically he only does so in order to deceive and mislead Bonario. In fact, it is Bonario's own family he is trying to divide, and Bonario himself whom he is attempting to have disinherited. Bonario is too trusting, and is only too willing to believe good of Mosca. In the world of *Volpone* goodness and innocence are not enough. Both Bonario and Celia are defenceless against the villainy of Mosca and Volpone. A naive trust in the goodness of human nature is no answer to cunning and duplicity, particularly when Vice is posing as Virtue. Indeed, in this scene, Mosca uses Bonario's good qualities: his willingness to believe the best of people, his trust and goodness, against him.

His real motives in his apparently altruistic actions are to sow discord in the relationship between Bonario and his father. In the play natural and normal feelings, such as the love and respect between father and son, are under attack from the unnatural and perverted instincts of Mosca and Volpone. Mosca, in particular, cannot bear goodness and virtue in others, perhaps because it reminds him of his own depraved nature, and he does his best to bring about the downfall of the only two good characters in the play, Bonario and Celia, through their innocence and trust.

Act III, Scene iii

Summary
The scene is set in Volpone's house where he is surrounded by the freaks of his household, Nano, Androgyno and Castrone, in a parody of a normal family. Volpone is anxiously awaiting the return of Mosca who has gone to procure Celia for him. He calls for entertainment so that the time will pass more quickly. Nano the dwarf poses the question: which of them is best at pleasing Volpone? Castrone claims that he is. In response Nano proceeds to recite some doggerel verses in praise of dwarfs. This performance is interrupted by a knock at the door. Volpone immediately takes to his couch and sends Nano to find out who it is. He hopes that it is Mosca with the news for which he has been waiting. When Nano informs him that it is Lady Would-Be, he goes into a frenzy of revulsion. He is afraid that his loathing for Lady Would-Be will drive out his desire for Celia, and he longs for her departure.

Commentary
Volpone's household is a visible and physical manifestation of his perverted desires. Their purpose is to amuse and flatter him, and the childishness and foolishness of their behaviour is a parody of the behaviour of ordinary children. In their earlier appearance, in the second scene of the play, Androgyno the fool presented arguments for his superiority over the others; now it is the turn of the dwarf, and he replies to the fool's arguments. Consequently there is a sense of continuity in the scenes where Nano, Adrogyno and Castrone appear. The fact that Volpone takes pleasure in such absurd trifles indicates his petty nature and reveals another side of his character: he is childish and easily amused. In such scenes the playwright makes it

clear that Volpone is not a heroic character to be admired, but on the contrary is infantile in his obsessions and pleasures.

Act III, Scene iv

Summary
Lady Politic Would-Be enters and requests Nano to inform Volpone that she has arrived. Her next concern is that she is not revealing enough of her body. She criticises her maids for not dressing her properly and tells Nano to send one of her women to her. When she appears, Lady Would-Be reprimands her for the fact that her curls are out of place. Then she calls a second woman and asks her whether her head-dress has been done properly. The woman replies that one hair is sticking out a little. Lady Would-Be mocks her and says that she has often preached to them about the necessity of frequently dressing her hair. In an aside Nano points out that Lady Politic Would-Be prizes her appearance more than fame or honour. Lady Would-Be goes on to say how she has told them that this knowledge of hairdressing will be a large dowry to them, enabling them to get noble husbands when they return to England. She is worried that the Italians will say that she cannot dress herself and that would be a fine thing to say about her country. She finishes her speech by complaining that her make-up has been applied too thickly.

Volpone is not pleased to see her and he tells her that he has had a dream in which a strange Fury entered his house. Instead of perceiving that this is a dig at her (she is incredibly thick-skinned), she begins to tell Volpone about one of her dreams, but cannot remember it. Effortlessly her conversation switches from dreams to cures for sickness, without pausing or hesitating. She offers to make Volpone a poultice, which he refuses. Lady Would-Be is a dilettante and has a superficial knowledge of many subjects. Her conversation now moves on to her study of medicine, music and painting, in rapid succession. She also says that a lady should be able to discourse, to write and to paint. In passing she manages to drop the names of Plato and Pythagoras with reference to their views on music. She concludes by turning to what she considers to be the female sex's 'chiefest ornament', which she believes to be 'In face, in voice, and clothes'. She thus manages to trivialise everything that she has mentioned before. In an effort to stop her flow of words, Volpone mentions that an ancient Greek poet has said that the highest female quality is silence. This is to no avail, for her immediate reply is to ask which poet, for she has read them all.

Volpone longs for her tongue to be still, but unabashed, Lady Would-Be continues to show off her knowledge of literature, saying that the English writers have stolen from Montaigne, Dante and

Aretino. When Volpone announces that his mind is agitated she replies that in such cases people must cure themselves, and she goes on to describe how this can be done by the use of reason and by changing the subject. Having exhausted him with her talkativeness, she next says that she must visit him more often for the sake of his health, which is the last thing that Volpone wants. She bores the sham invalid still further by beginning an account of a companion of her youth, a man who would listen for three or four hours while she talked. It is plain to Volpone and the audience that he was just as bored as Volpone is. The invalid cries out in desperation to be rescued from his visitor.

Commentary
From her very first appearance it is clear that Lady Would-Be, just like her husband, is a comic character. The audience's attitude towards her has been prepared by Volpone's speech at the end of the previous scene. She is obsessed with her appearance and is concerned that she is not showing off enough of her body. She is also critical of her serving women for not dressing her properly and because her curls are out of place. Nano comments in an aside:

> . . . Anon, she'll beat her women
> Because her nose is red. (15–16)

When she reprimands her women the language she uses is from formal rhetoric and argument: 'Read you the principles', 'argued all the grounds'. The employment of these terms, normally used in serious intellectual debate, in the frivolous context of hairdressing, creates a comic effect. The audience must be alert to Jonson's use of language to appreciate the play fully. There is also an intentional pun on 'dressing' which is repeated several times in this scene. 'Dressing' can apply not only to hairdressing, but also to telling someone off, which is what Lady Would-Be is doing.

It is clear that Lady Would-Be is an extremely superficial person who places more importance on her appearance than anything else. Speaking of the Italians she calls them 'curious', which means both 'particular' and also 'inquisitive'. She is worried that the Italians will say that she cannot dress herself and that would be a poor reflection on her country. This is all highly ironical when we remember Peregrine's speech to her husband, when he is surprised that she has come to Italy to study the Venetian courtesans' way of dressing their hair, their fashions and their way of behaving. Jonson's intention is humorous, in suggesting that a respectable English lady should study prostitutes to learn behaviour and how to dress.

Lady Would-Be is garrulous, her conversation darting about from subject to subject. She is a forerunner of Mrs Malaprop in Sheridan's play, *The Rivals*, in her ability to mangle the English language and to use the wrong word with a similar sound to the one she intends. She says 'the golden mediocrity' when she intends to say 'the golden mean,' thus saying the opposite of what she intends to signify. Her conversation switches effortlessly from subject to subject without pause or hesitation, so that Volpone's response is to say in an aside: 'Another flood of words! a very torrent.'

Jonson completes her character by making her a dilettante, and she tries to show off her knowledge of many subjects, ranging from medicine and music to painting. She is the only one of the legacy hunters that Volpone is not happy to see, and the only one who makes him suffer in his disguise as an invalid, so that he cries out: 'Some power, some fate, some fortune rescue me!'

Act III, Scene v

Summary
As if in answer to his master's prayers, Mosca enters and Volpone begs him to get rid of Lady Would-Be and her talkativeness. Mosca asks if she has given a present yet. But Volpone does not care; all he wants is to be rid of her. It transpires that Lady Would-Be has made a cap to give to Volpone as a present. This offering is unlikely to endear her to him when compared with the value of the other gifts. Mosca rapidly gets rid of her by telling her that he has seen her husband in a gondola with the most cunning courtesan in Venice. On hearing this she leaves. Mosca tells Volpone that all his hopes are maturing. Corbaccio is bringing his new will (naming him as his heir and disinheriting his son Bonario). Volpone regains his spirits and looks forward to his encounter with Celia.

Commentary
The comedy created by the character of Lady Would-Be continues in this scene when Volpone voices his wish to be rid of her:

> Oh,
> Rid me of this torture quickly, there;
> My madam with the everlasting voice; (3–4)

Part of the irony of the situation is that Volpone has been driven to such desperation by her that he no longer cares whether she gives him a present or not. In addition, the present of the cap indicates that as well as her talkativeness, Lady Would-Be has another vice: meanness. Mosca, as usual, understands how to get rid of her, showing once more that he is adept at manipulating people. He uses her jealousy of her husband to ensure that she leaves immediately.

Act III, Scene vi

Summary

Bonario enters Volpone's house with Mosca so that he can overhear his father and Volpone. Mosca tells him to hide and informs him that it is his father knocking at the door, so that he is forced to leave him. Bonario, still unable to believe that his father is planning to disinherit him, conceals himself.

Commentary

Jonson's use of two short scenes – scene vi is the shortest scene in the play – speeds up the action so that it verges on farce. This scene is extremely important to the outcome of the play, because it is the concealed Bonario who secretly observes Volpone's attempt to rape Celia, and who prevents it.

Act III, Scene vii

Summary

Mosca expresses alarm when he discovers that instead of Corbaccio it is Corvino and Celia who are at the door, and he upbraids Corvino for his premature arrival, saying that he told him that he would send for him. Corvino replies that he was frightened that Mosca might forget and that the other legacy hunters would forestall them. Mosca is amazed at Corvino's haste to cuckold himself. It becomes apparent from Corvino's conversation with Celia that he has not yet informed her of the purpose of their visit. He does so out of earshot of the audience. Meanwhile Mosca turns his attention to Bonario, lets him know that it will be half an hour before his father arrives, and invites him to wait in the gallery where there are some books with which to pass the time.

Corvino and Celia continue their conversation within the hearing of the audience. Corvino insists that Celia should go to bed with Volpone. She mistakenly believes that he is testing her faithfulness. Like Bonario she is virtuous and naive; she cannot deal with the evil that exists around her, and is powerless before it. She begs Corvino to lock her up for ever, for she believes that he is acting out of jealousy to test her. Corvino insists that he means what he says and he asks her to show herself to be an obedient wife. He reminds her that he has given her reasons: what the physicians have said, how much it concerns him, what his financial obligations are, and how his financial resources are inadequate to save him. He adds that if she is loyal to him she will help him with his enterprise. (It seems that Corvino is in financial difficulties and this is the reason for his eagerness to get his hands on Volpone's wealth, even at the cost of prostituting his own wife.)

Celia asks him if she is to respect this venture even to the detriment of his honour and he replies that honour is of no importance. Evidently Corvino's greed is stronger than his sense of honour. Corvino emphasises Volpone's feebleness and concludes by asking: 'And what can this man hurt you?' She is amazed by this sudden and complete change in him. He goes on to say that reputation is a trifle; no one else will know what she has done apart from Volpone, who is incapable of speaking, and Mosca who is in his pocket. Celia demands whether heaven and earth mean nothing, asks him to be jealous still and to emulate the saints and hate sin. His response is that if he thought it was a sin he would not ask her to do it; it is a charitable act for a medical purpose. Celia is horrified and asks how heaven can suffer such a change.

Volpone himself is delighted at what is taking place and praises Mosca for his part in it. Corvino now drags the unwilling Celia towards the bed and Mosca tells his master that Corvino has come to offer his wife to him. The parasite delights in the depravity to which he has brought Corvino. Volpone, still feigning sickness, tells him to thank Corvino, but his kindness is in vain because he is past helping. He asks Corvino to pray for him and to use his fortune with reverence, implying that he has made Corvino his heir.

Celia still refuses to go to Volpone and, when Corvino threatens her with violence, she replies that she would rather do anything: even take poison. He threatens to drag her by the hair through the streets and proclaim her to be a loose woman. He also threatens to cut her face with a knife, and goes on to say that he will buy a slave whom he will kill and tie to her, and devise a monstrous crime, the name of which he will burn into her skin in capital letters. Corvino believes that Celia is afraid of the shame attached, and not of the deed of infidelity itself. It is for this reason that he threatens her with public exposure as a harlot. When the threat of making false accusations against her in public fails, he tries to bribe her with promises of jewels and clothes. All she has to do is to kiss Volpone. He wants to know why she is trying to undo him and disgrace him. When he fails to get her to do what he wants, Corvino proceeds to abuse her verbally. Mosca advises him to leave his wife alone with Volpone because with her husband absent she may be more forthcoming. Corvino and Mosca go out and leave Celia alone with Volpone.

She calls upon God and his angels to help her and asks where shame has gone, that men can so easily put off honour, and value it less than money. With the disappearance of the others, Volpone springs to life, speaks to Celia, and leaps off his couch. He assures her that Corvino is not worthy of her love because he would sell her merely for hope of gain. He asks her why she is amazed to see him revive and divulges that it was for her sake that he disguised himself as a mountebank, in order to see her at her window. Volpone has now thrown caution to the winds in his desire to possess Celia, showing and telling her quite plainly that he is as fit and healthy as when he was younger and acted the part of Antinous, and attracted all the ladies. In his attempt to seduce her he sings the song 'Come, my Celia let us prove'. Her response is to ask lightning to strike her face. He assures her that she has found a worthy lover in place of her base husband. He offers her his entire fortune and in a series of luxuriant and vibrant images, calculated to appeal with their visual splendour, attempts to buy her. He offers her a rope of pearls, a ruby and a priceless diamond. Then appealing to her appetite for food, he offers her a meal composed of parts of exotic birds. Celia's reply to this is that some could be moved by such delights, but she, who considers her innocence the only thing worth having, cannot be caught by such sensual baits. She appeals to Volpone's conscience.

Volpone disregards her plea, and in his sustained attempt at seduction offers her more and more delicacies and exotic pleasures. The long list of extravagances which he proposes ends with his suggesting that they should drink gold and amber. He offers to have Nano, Castrone and Adrogyno entertain her and suggests that they make love disguised as various Greek gods and goddesses, as well as in several kinds of contemporary costume. (Volpone takes a delight in disguise and dressing up and it seems this extends even to erotic play.) He concludes the song to Celia by saying that others will be jealous of them when they discover the number of their orgasms.

Celia's reply to these blandishments is to beg him to spare her. But Volpone is deaf to her entreaties and threatens to rape her if she does not yield to him. Bonario, who has heard everything, leaps out from hiding and commands him to free Celia on pain of death. He also accuses him of being an impostor, and says he would kill him immediately, but that he is unwilling to take the law into his own hands. He tells Celia that they will leave the den of villainy and that Volpone will shortly receive his just reward. Volpone is reduced to despair by the sudden and unexpected appearance of Bonario. He calls on the roof to fall on him and bury him, because he has been unmasked and betrayed to beggary and infamy.

Commentary
This is the central scene of the play and the turning-point for the main action and the fortunes of the characters in the main plot. Up to this point the legacy hunters have behaved according to Mosca's and Volpone's plans, but the unexpected arrival of Corvino signals their increasing loss of control over events. There is also the intrusion of the outside world into Volpone's closed world, in the

person of Bonario, who enters and disrupts it. In this scene Volpone's fortunes suffer a complete reversal. When it opens it seems that his desire for Celia is about to be satisfied, and it ends with his exposure and apparent ruin. Jonson shows consummate skill in the development of the plot and his introduction of complication of the action in order to sustain and increase the interest of his audience.

Corvino's reasons for prostituting his wife to Volpone are based on financial considerations and he asks Celia to respect his 'venture' which at the time that Jonson was writing meant a commercial enterprise in which there is considerable risk; even today speculators talk of 'venture capital'. Part of Jonson's satire is therefore directed at Corvino's belief that his legacy hunting is a commercial venture, and in addition he is satirising Corvino's profession, which is that of merchant.

> CORVINO Honour? tut, a breath;
> There's no such thing in nature – a mere term
> Invented to awe fools. What is my gold
> The worse, for touching? clothes, for being looked on?
> Why, this's no more. (38–40)

There is considerable irony in Jonson's presentation of Corvino and he goes on to reveal far more of the character of the man who previously appeared as the archetypal jealous husband in II.v, where he mercilessly abused Celia for merely looking out of the window. His views on honour have shifted radically. He now portrays the prostitution of his own wife as no more harmful than having his gold touched. This adds to the reification effect of the play, in which Celia is portrayed as a passive female object to be exchanged among the male characters. The fact that she is being sold in return for gold is made quite explicit here. The gold imagery, which Jonson introduced in Volpone's opening speech, contributes a great deal to the meaning of the drama in which commercial values replace and override the accepted Christian values of the time.

The speech also records how values were shifting from those of a feudal society, with its concept of honour, to those of one based on profit. The growth of capitalism in England in the seventeenth century paved the way for the Industrial Revolution in the eighteenth. Jonson's implied views are those of a conservative who did not welcome the growing capitalist economy or the change in values which it entailed. In the poem 'To Penshurst', written in praise of the way of life of a large country house, Jonson lamented the passing of the hereditary nobility with its feudal order and hospitality and contrasted this with the empty, newly constructed and ostentatious buildings of the *nouveau riche*, who made their money from trade and monopolies, and did not preserve the ancient way of life.

Other contemporary dramatists also attacked the greedy and rapacious City man without hereditary or feudal rank, as did Massinger, for example, in his *A New Way to Pay Old Debts*, in the person of Sir Giles Overreach.

Celia's replies to her husband's entreaties make it plain that Corvino is disregarding Christian constraints on behaviour: all that concerns him is whether other people know about it.

> CELIA   Are heaven and saints then nothing?
> Will they be blind, or stupid? (53–4)

Celia's reply to her husband is couched in terms of Christian belief. In the context of Volpone's world, however, conventional Christian ideology as exemplified by Celia is ineffectual, and he ignores her pleas.

The ease with which Corvino puts away his former jealousy is quite remarkable. As in other scenes in the play, Mosca and Volpone make a correct moral assessment of the motives and actions of their victims. Mosca's comments as he brings Corvino and Celia to Volpone's bedside, point out the truth of the situation:

> MOSCA   Sir, Signior Corvino, here, is come to see you –
> VOLPONE   Oh!
> MOSCA   And hearing of the consultation had
> So lately for your health, is come to offer,
> Or rather, sir, to prostitute . . . (71–74)

This is the lowest moral point of the play and it is reflected in the language that Mosca uses to describe Corvino's behaviour.

When his arguments seem to have no effect on Celia, Corvino turns to vicious threats. There is heavy irony in that he threatens her with exposure for the very thing he is asking her to do, namely, to act as a prostitute which she would be if she did what he asked. Jonson adds to the contradictions of the situation when, after unsuccessfully trying to bribe her with jewellery and new clothes, Corvino asks: 'Will you disgrace me thus? Do you thirst for my undoing?' It is Corvino himself who is disgracing himself and bringing about his own undoing. This irony is added to a few lines later when he says:

> 'Sdeath, if she would but speak to him,
> And save my reputation, 'twere somewhat;
> But spitefully to affect my utter ruin! (122–4)

With the exit of Corvino and Mosca Celia is left alone with Volpone for the central confrontation of the play, between herself representing Virtue and Volpone representing Vice. Volpone places himself in danger of exposure because of his desire for her. The twentieth-century reader who is unaware of the extent to which Jonson used the art of rhetoric, will take Volpone's speeches at their face value of vivid and eloquent poetry. If we remember, however, that the purpose behind his speeches is to persuade Celia to go to bed with him, we can see them as examples of the use of rhetoric.

Volpone does not attempt to seduce Celia by the use of logic or by making a rational appeal; he tries to sway her emotions by appealing to all of her senses and by the use of an ornate and hyperbolic style, loaded with figures of speech. He begins by denigrating his rival for her affections, her husband, then describes the efforts he has made to see her, because of her beauty. He attempts to overcome any possible dislike she might have for his supposed invalid condition by stating that he is, in fact, extremely vigorous. The next stage in his attempt at seduction is to use the power of music and song to move her. The song 'Come, my Celia let us prove' has appeared in many anthologies and is one of Jonson's most famous poems. It shows Jonson at his best, with its precise poetic diction and its strong lyrical grace. In fact it is an adaptation of a poem to Lesbia by the Roman poet Catullus. However, by giving this beautiful lyric to the unscrupulous Volpone, in his attempt to seduce the virtuous Celia, Jonson produces a somewhat paradoxical effect.

This also indicates an ambivalent attitude in Jonson towards the seducer's use of poetry. We find a similar ambivalence in the Puritan poet, John Milton, in the masque *Comus*, where the character Comus is given the best poetry in his attempt to seduce the Lady, and in the character of Satan in *Paradise Lost*. There was a growing suspicion of poetic language in the seventeenth century, and the suppression of figurative language and the encouragement of a more plain style was part of the Puritan project.

Volpone tells Celia that in place of a 'base husband' she has found a 'worthy lover', so using the rhetorical device of antithesis. Volpone offers her his entire fortune in an attempt to buy her. He does this skilfully by appealing to her visual sense in a profusion of extravagant images of pearls and precious stones. The next of her senses he appeals to is that of taste and he offers her a meal composed of parts of outlandish birds culminating in the legendary phoenix.

Celia's reply to Volpone is in pure and unadorned language, in contrast to his speeches of seduction:

> Good sir, these things might move a mind affected
> With such delights; but I, whose innocence
> Is all I can think wealthy, or worth th'enjoying,
> And which once lost, I have naught to lose beyond it,
> Cannot be taken with these sensual baits.
> If you have conscience . . . (206–11)

This is the most powerful scene of the play in its confrontation between Good and Evil. In answer to Volpone's luxurious entice-ments Celia opposes her innocence and virtue. Volpone represents all the joys of excess: Celia those of moderation. Volpone offers her the seductive pleasures of earthly delights: Celia opposes them with the pallid consolations of conventional morality.

In his extended attempt at seduction Volpone offers her more and more arcane pleasures:

> Thy baths shall be the juice of July-flowers
> Spirit of roses, and of violets,
> The milk of unicorns, and panthers' breath
> Gathered in bags, and mixed with Cretan wines,
> Our drink shall be prepared gold and amber; (213–17)

The long series of sybaritic delights ends with the proposal that they should actually drink gold. In the play gold is invested with a special significance by Volpone, and in suggesting that they drink it, he is making her what he believes to be the highest offer he can. The richness and extravagance of the gifts that Volpone proposes to shower on Celia lend the verse that he speaks a richness and vitality denied to Celia's plaintive moralising. This ambivalence towards the effect of metaphorical language in poetry reflects a tension in Jonson himself, between the middle class Puritan values of restraint, and the aristocratic ones of extravagance and display. The conflict between these two sets of values was one of the aspects of the class conflict within English society which was to lead to what Christopher Hill and recent historians call the English Revolution, with the execution of Charles and the victory of the Parliamentarians. The success of the Puritan project was exemplified by the activities of the Royal Society in its attempt to purify English by ridding it of figurative language, and to promote the growth of science through promulgating the views of Francis Bacon.

The unhealthy nature of Volpone's epicureanism is indicated by his wish that they should make love in various disguises. A large element in Volpone's character is his love of play-acting. He enjoys adopting disguises, as when he pretends to be the mountebank Scoto; he also takes pleasure from his performance as an invalid which hoodwinks the legacy hunters; and finally, he refers to his younger self playing the part of Antinous. His exhibitionism even extends to imagining spectators watching Celia and him making love.

With the failure of his rhetoric to persuade Celia to go to bed with him he shows another side of his nature. He is prepared to descend to rape. Bonario's sudden and unexpected appearance prevents this, but Bonario is not presented uncritically by Jonson, for his use of language is pompous and almost laughable, and inevitably affects the way the audience perceives him:

> Forbear, foul ravisher! libidinous swine!
> Free the forced lady, or thou diest, impostor. (267–8)

However, Bonario has correctly observed Volpone's obsession with, and deification of gold, when he says; 'Before this altar, and this dross, thy idol.' Jonson's use of language is extremely specific here. The *Shorter Oxford English Dictionary* gives for 'dross': 'the scum thrown off from metals in smelting', and we appreciate that Jonson's choice of language is both exact and appropriate.

Act III, Scene viii

Summary
After the complete failure of his scheming, which was to culminate in Volpone's seduction of Celia, Mosca enters bleeding – he has been wounded by Bonario. This is the low point of the plotters' fortunes so far, because Volpone is in grave danger of being exposed, both for his attempted rape of Celia and for the confidence trick he has been working on the would-be heirs. In order to temper Volpone's possible anger at the disastrous results of his schemes, Mosca immediately accepts the blame and expresses surprise that Bonario has managed to overhear Volpone's attempted seduction and rape of Celia. To mollify Volpone still further, Mosca melodramatically offers to allow Volpone to exact retribution upon him, and finally he makes the somewhat ridiculous suggestion that they should commit suicide together. There is knocking at the door and Volpone's guilty conscience makes him believe that police officers have come to arrest him. Mosca, master of the situation as ever, tells Volpone to return to his sick-bed. Then, to his surprise, he discovers that it is only Corbaccio at the door.

Commentary
In this scene Mosca proves himself to be as successful at manipulating his master as he is with the fortune hunters. Not only was he responsible for initiating the scheme to seduce Celia, but he also admitted Bonario to the house so that he was able to overhear Volpone and Celia, and so made it possible for Volpone to be exposed. Despite this, he manages with ease to placate his patron. He does this by instantly accepting all the blame for what has happened, thus deflecting Volpone's possible anger. Also noticeable in his speeches is the high frequency of 'sirs' he obsequiously addresses to him. Volpone is curiously passive in this scene and it is Mosca who keeps his wits about him and, when there is knocking at the door, urges Volpone to return to his couch, to maintain the pretence that he is ill. Mosca thus proves that he is more in command of the

situation than his master, and this leads to his growing independence of action, and his underestimation of Volpone.

Act III, Scene ix

Summary
Corbaccio enters, and at the same time Voltore sneaks in, unseen by the others. When he finds that it is only Corbaccio at the door, Mosca manages to turn events to his and Volpone's advantage. He informs Corbaccio that his son Bonario has come to the house with drawn sword, looking for him, because of his desire to make Volpone his heir. Believing Mosca's lies about his son, Corbaccio is outraged. Mosca sees that his falsification of events has fallen on fertile ground and expands his story further by adding that Bonario has also vowed to kill Volpone. Corbaccio, gullible as ever, says that this act will indeed disinherit him, and hands over to Mosca his will, which names Volpone as his heir instead of his son. Corbaccio asks whether Volpone will die soon, revealing his predatory nature. Mosca replies that he is afraid he will outlast May. Because he is hard of hearing, Corbaccio mishears this and asks Mosca 'Today?' Mosca repeats what he has said and Corbaccio suggests that Mosca should give him a fatal dose of medicine.

Voltore has overheard the entire exchange between Mosca and Corbaccio, and reveals his understanding of what is going on by saying in an aside that he sees that Mosca is a knave. Voltore now makes his presence known to Mosca, who wonders, also in an aside, whether Voltore had overheard him. Voltore shouts 'Parasite!' at him, indicating that he has indeed eavesdropped on the conversation. Mosca pretends not to hear this accurate insult, and welcomes Voltore. Voltore sarcastically confronts him with his duplicity and double-dealing, but Mosca feigns innocence and Voltore asks him what is the device about a will he has heard him talking about with Corbaccio. Mosca is equal to the situation and pretends that it has all been a plot for the good of Voltore. He says that he told Bonario of his father's attempt to disinherit him, and hid him in the house to hear it, in the hope that the unnaturalness of the act would enrage him to the point that he would physically attack his father. Bonario would then be apprehended by the law, thus leaving Voltore not only the heir to Volpone's fortune, but also that of Corbaccio. Blinded by greed, Voltore readily accepts Mosca's lies. Mosca has skilfully used all the events to his and Volpone's advantage, thus demonstrating, once more, his quick-wittedness and his ability to get people to do what he wants.

Encouraged by the ease with which he has made Voltore believe his lies about Corbaccio and Bonario, Mosca now makes him swallow another story to explain away Volpone's attempted rape of Celia, and to put the blame on Bonario. He tells Voltore that Bonario grew impatient with waiting and rushed out, seized Celia, wounded him, made her swear on pain of death that Volpone had raped her, and took her off with him to accuse his father, defame Volpone and defeat Voltore. Effortlessly Mosca thus switches the blame to Bonario. Voltore tells Mosca to fetch Celia's husband, Corvino, and to bring him to the Law Courts, in order to stop Bonario. Mosca, persuaded of the success of his machinations, praises Voltore and repeats that he has done everything for his good. Corbaccio overhears their conversation, but Mosca easily deals with him by pretending that he was merely asking him to leave, and Corbaccio and Voltore go out together. It seems that Mosca has extricated both his master and himself from their difficult situation, and he asks Volpone to pray for their success.

Commentary
Jonson shows great dramatic skill in his management of a complicated plot and also in the way he extracts humour from Corbaccio's deafness, while revealing his underlying ruthlessness and unscrupulousness. Mosca himself is now threatened with exposure because he has been overheard by Voltore, just as previously it was Volpone who was overheard by a third party, Bonario. The parasite skilfully incorporates what Voltore has overheard, namely that Corbaccio is making out his will in Volpone's favour, into the general lie that he is doing everything for Voltore's ultimate good. The twists and turns of the plot at this juncture, as the playwright adds complication to complication, show Jonson to be a master of situation comedy.

The theme of unnatural behaviour runs through the play. This aspect of Corbaccio's action in disinheriting his own son in favour of Volpone is evoked by Mosca's 'the unnaturalness of the act', and this adds to our sense that the greed of the fortune hunters is against nature.

Act IV, Scene i

Summary
The act opens with Sir Politic Would-Be talking to Peregrine about the incident in which Volpone, disguised as a mountebank, was beaten away by Corvino. Typically, Sir Politic has interpreted this as a plot against himself. He tries to impress Peregrine as a seasoned traveller and offers him advice and some details which he has set down specifically about the region. He instructs him that his demeanour should be grave and reserved so as to give nothing away, and that he should be extremely cautious in what he says and the

company he keeps. He concludes with the extraordinary advice never to speak the truth, and expands on this by saying that this applies when speaking to foreigners, for it is they whom he will speak with most frequently. He warns him to keep himself to himself, otherwise he will be cheated hourly. Throughout this passage he voices the suspicions of the Englishman travelling abroad. He advises Peregrine to profess no religion but to wonder at the diversity of all and to say that the laws of the land are enough for him.

To further impress Peregrine, Sir Politic pretends an easy familiarity with the writings of both Machiavelli and Bodin, and without pausing for breath tells him to learn how to use a fork at meals and to know the correct time of day to eat melons and figs. Mocking him, Peregrine asks if knowing when he must eat his melon and figs is a question of diplomacy too. The gullible Sir Politic replies that for the Venetians it is, because if there is anything preposterous about a man they will sum him up immediately and expose him. He boasts to Peregrine that he has lived in Venice for fourteen months, and that from his first week everyone took him for a citizen of Venice, because he knew the external forms of behaviour so well.

The wandering knight now begins to describe his schemes for getting rich quick. One of these is a far-fetched project to import herrings from Rotterdam to Venice, which he is sure will make him a profit. He goes on to say that he has more important schemes which he hopes to suggest to the Great Council of Venice. One of these concerns tinder-boxes (which were common in Venice at the time, and were small enough to be carried in a pocket). Sir Politic believes that they constitute a threat to the Arsenal of Venice, where arms and amunition are stored. His suggestion is that only known and patriotic citizens should be allowed to have them at home, and that they should be registered and only of a size not to be easily concealed. His next hare-brained scheme is to use onions for detecting the plague on ships arriving from the East. He also lets Peregrine know that he keeps a diary, which Peregrine asks to see, and from which he reads some of the entries aloud. The diary is full of trivia and nonsense and includes details of Sir Politic's most intimate personal habits.

Commentary

The fourth act returns to the sub-plot concerning Sir Politic Would-Be. The sub-plot is again seen to act not only as comic relief from the more serious main plot, but also to imitate it in several important ways, acting both as a counterpoint to and ironic commentary on it. Jonson has already established the English knight as a figure of fun from his initial appearance in II,i, and this scene adds more idiosyncrasies to his characterisation. One of the ways that the sub-plot mirrors the main plot is that Sir Politic is attempting to mislead

Peregrine, in order to create a false impression of himself, just as Volpone is trying to mislead all the suitors. The difference is that while Sir Politic is an innocent and harmless person pretending to be cunning and worldly-wise, Volpone and Mosca are cunning and evil characters pretending to be innocent.

In his efforts to impress Peregrine with his experience as a traveller and man of the world, the wayfaring knight offers him some strange advice, 'beware you never speak a truth'. Ironically this dictum is more closely followed by Mosca than by anyone else in the play. Sir Politic himself is an innocent abroad, in spite of his pretence of shrewdness. In his rapid leaps from subject to subject he demonstrates that, like his wife, he has a grasshopper mind, and just like her he is more interested in the trivial niceties of Venetian behaviour than in anything more profound.

The audience's perception of Sir Politic as half-crazed increases as he unfolds his lunatic schemes for getting rich quick, in which Jonson is also poking fun at the acquisitiveness of the merchant class. Sir Politic's obsession with the possible use of tinder-boxes to blow up the Arsenal is an oblique reference to Guy Fawkes's unsuccessful attempt to blow up the Houses of Parliament a year previously, in 1605. It had to be oblique because Jonson himself was a Catholic at the time, and England was swept by a wave of anti-Catholic hysteria as a result of the Gunpowder Plot. Jonson is also poking fun at the national paranoia and the belief at the time that all Catholics were traitors. He does this by presenting as ridiculous Sir Politic's fearfulness about tinder-boxes:

> Advertise to the state, how fit it were,
> That none but such as were known patriots,
> Sound lovers of their country, should be suffered
> T'enjoy them in their houses; and even those
> Sealed at some office, and at such a bigness,
> As might not lurk in pockets. (94–9)

Sir Politic's idea to use onions for detecting the plague includes word-play on 'waterworks', a joke which survives even today and, according to the *Shorter Oxford English Dictionary*, can also mean 'to make water'. Sir Politic resembles Volpone in that he too is full of schemes for making money. The difference is that all his schemes are crack-brained and harmless, whereas Mosca's and Volpone's schemes involve defrauding others. Thus he acts as a double of and an ironic counterpart to the main character of the play.

Through his portrayal of Sir Politic Would-Be in this scene, Jonson is mocking the vogue for travel to the continent which existed at the time. He is also satirising the English travellers of his day, some of whom wrote books about their experiences. Lastly, he is ridiculing

and subverting the whole genre of travel writing. He does this by
showing Sir Politic's passion for noting down the most insignificant
details, even about his most personal habits. For example, he reveals
an obsessive interest in his bodily functions, when he records that 'at
St Mark's, I urined'. The fact that he recorded this, in connection
with his experiences at one of the most famous and beautiful squares
in Europe, indicates the level of his appreciation, and by implication
that of other travellers and their accounts. With his worthless and
excruciatingly funny notes, about which Peregrine makes the ironical
comment 'Faith, these are politic notes', Sir Peregrine is presented as
the epitome of the eccentric and foolish Englishman abroad.

Act IV, Scene ii

Summary
Lady Would-Be enters at a distance with Nano and her two women,
looking for her husband. Despite her anxiety to catch her husband in
the company of the courtesan, she is worried that the heat will do her
complexion more harm than Sir Politic is worth. One of her women
spots him talking to Peregrine and informs her. Lady Would-Be
immediately assumes that Peregrine is a prostitute disguised in men's
clothing. Sir Politic has also seen his wife; he points her out to
Peregrine and proceeds to praise her. They all meet and Sir Politic
introduces Peregrine to Lady Would-Be. She reprimands her husband for his supposed scandalous behaviour, and goes on to mock
Peregrine, calling him 'Master-Would-Be'. She first says that she is
unwilling to have public argument with any gentlewoman, and then
proceeds to do just that. She insults Peregrine, calling him a eunuch
and a hermaphrodite. Sir Politic tries to defend Peregrine, but his
wife insists that he is a prostitute and 'A female devil in a male
outside'. Gullible Sir Politic accepts what his wife is saying and
informs Peregrine that he must bid farewell to him.

Lady Would-Be makes one of her amusing slips of the tongue,
accusing her husband of 'carnival concupiscence' instead of 'carnal
concupiscence'. Then in a fury she seizes the clothing of Peregrine
who, in return, asks her whether her husband has sent her to beg
shirts or to invite him home. She retorts: 'This cannot work you out
of my snare', while still holding on to his clothing. Peregrine wonders
aloud, if he is in her snare. He returns her insults, and tells her that
her nose is red on one side, and this infuriates her even more.

Commentary
This scene, with its comic effects relying on mistaken identity, is one
of the most humorous of the play. After the previous scene in which
Jonson fully displayed the character of Sir Politic, the author now

shows the audience his equally comic wife. We are made aware of Lady Would-Be's vanity: she is more worried about the effects of the heat on her complexion than on catching up with her straying husband. The sub-plot echoes the main plot: Lady Would-Be tries to unmask Peregrine, just as Celia and Bonario have unmasked Volpone. Lady Would-Be reveals the contrariness of her nature by first saying that she is unwilling to have a public argument with any gentlewoman and then proceeding to have one with Peregrine. She flies at him, and the insults she heaps on him are scathing in the extreme: she calls him a eunuch and a hermaphrodite. This also echoes the main plot; it will be remembered that Volpone kept both a hermaphrodite and a eunuch for his amusement. Lady Would-Be also displays her propensity for making slips of the tongue. The scene is both an ironic commentary on the main action and comic in its own right, providing a breathing-space from the main action.

Act IV, Scene iii

Summary
At this point Mosca, who is responsible for Lady Would-Be's mistake over Peregrine's identity, comes up. She tells him that she has caught the whore he told her about, disguised. Mosca, feigning innocence, says that the whore has already been apprehended, and that Peregrine is a young gentleman who has only arrived in Venice that morning. Lady Would-Be realises her mistake and apologises to Peregrine, who is astonished at her sudden change of mood. She begs him to forget her anger and issues an invitation to him to 'use her' if he remains in Venice. Lady Would-Be again manages to convey a meaning she does not intend, for the implication of her remark is that she is prepared to go to bed with him. The joke continues when she goes on to say, 'Pray you, sir, use me, the more you see me, the more I shall conceive,' before departing. Peregrine is astonished at her remarks and believes that Sir Politic is trying to prostitute his wife to him, which of course is not the case. In addition, he mistakenly believes that Sir Politic has taken advantage of his inexperience, and resolves to test the knight's supposed experience to see if it is proof against a counter-plot.

Commentary
Lady Would-Be's character is developed still further, and there is the suggestion that her morals are not all that they should be. Her slips of the tongue also lead Peregrine to imagine that her husband is acting as a pimp. Again there are echoes of the main plot, where Corvino has attempted to persuade his wife to go to bed with Volpone. This in turn makes Peregrine determine to play a joke on Sir Politic to test

him. The scene is crucial to the development of the sub-plot because much that occurs subsequently has its origins here. It also echoes several elements in the main plot in a humorous way: the unmasking of someone who is disguised (in the main plot Volpone's unmasking, and in the sub-plot Lady Would-Be's attempt to unmask Peregrine); a husband acting as pander to his wife (in the main plot Corvino, and in the sub-plot, apparently, Sir Politic); and finally the attempt to mislead someone (in the main plot to defraud the legacy hunters, in the sub-plot to bring Sir Politic to his senses).

Act IV, Scene iv

Summary
We find Voltore, Corbaccio, Corvino and Mosca at the Scrutineo, or court, preparing to make false accusations against Bonario and Celia. Mosca has just primed the others with the lie that they must all stick to, if their evidence is to appear consistent in court. Corvino is worried that their advocate, Voltore, has been told the truth about his attempt to prostitute Celia, but Mosca reassures him, saying that he has been told a lie which will save his reputation. Mosca openly shows his contempt for Corbaccio and Corvino. He urges Voltore on with the case, telling him that he will be the only one to benefit, and in addition he mentions that he has another witness he can produce.

Commentary
Mosca's scheming has reached a new level. He now persuades the legacy hunters to perjure themselves in the hope of future gain. Their readiness to make false accusations against the innocent Bonario and Celia reveal the extent to which their greed has overcome all moral scruples. Voltore, as their advocate, will argue their case in court. Mosca shows his distaste for the legacy hunters; he calls Corbaccio 'croaker' and Corvino 'buffalo' out of their hearing, but he flatters Voltore outrageously for his powers of oratory. Mosca's gulling of the fortune hunters has previously been conducted in private; now it is to take place in public, in open court. This movement from the private world of Volpone's house into the outside world also exposes Mosca and Volpone to grave danger. Volpone's world has been disturbed by the intruder Bonario; now both Volpone and Mosca risk public exposure.

Act IV, Scene v

Summary
The court officials enter with Bonario and Celia. The magistrates

have apparently been told what has been going on, for they are discussing the unnaturalness of the behaviour of Corbaccio and Corvino, and Volpone's fraudulent deception. It seems that the game is up. The first magistrate asks why Volpone is not in court and Mosca replies that he is too weak to come, but the magistrate insists, and officers are sent to fetch him. Voltore asks the court if he may speak for Volpone, and then declares that he will reveal the most shameless piece of impudence and treachery that ever shamed the Venetian state. He accuses Celia of having been an adulteress for a long time with Bonario and states that they were caught in the act by her husband Corvino, who forgave her. Instead of being grateful for this act of forgiveness they began to resent it. Corbaccio, hearing of this foul deed committed by his son, together with other crimes, decided to disinherit him. The magistrates are puzzled because Bonario has always had a good reputation. Voltore dismisses this by saying that his depravity is even more dangerous because he could deceive them so easily, under a pretence of being virtuous.

Voltore then says that, on the day he was to be disinherited, Bonario, in conspiracy with Celia, entered Volpone's house with the intention of murdering his own father. As Corbaccio was not there, Bonario dragged Volpone out naked from where he had lain bedridden for three years or more. Then he wounded Mosca in the face, and together with Celia, decided to stop his father making Volpone his heir, by discrediting him. They also hoped to redeem themselves by laying charges of infamy against Corvino, to whom they should both admit they owed their lives.

The first magistrate demands to know what proof they have of this, and Bonario asks that no credit should be given to Voltore's 'mercenary tongue'. Voltore calls Corbaccio to speak and when he tells the court that he disclaims his son, Bonario is astonished and cries out, 'Have they made you do this?' Corbaccio refuses to listen to him and insults him publicly. Bonario is a dutiful son and, rather than oppose his father, meekly sits down. Both Celia and Bonario seem powerless and defenceless against the evil that opposes them. Voltore next calls Corvino who proceeds to make false statements against his wife: 'This woman, please your fatherhood, is a whore'. Then he tells the court that he has seen Celia and Bonario together. Having exposed himself to public ridicule for being a cuckold, Corvino now foolishly asks Mosca, 'There is no shame in this now, is there?' Mosca of course replies, 'None.' Corvino then damns his wife as a whore and she faints, upon which Corvino heartlessly remarks, 'Rare, Prettily feigned! again!' Mosca is the next to be called, and he says that his wound, which he received aiding Volpone, speaks for him. According to Mosca Bonario did it because he failed to find his father when Celia, who was well rehearsed, received her cue to cry rape.

Bonario protests that this is carefully plotted and shameless audacity, but the magistrates begin to doubt Bonario and Celia's version of events. Voltore accuses Celia of being a brazen prostitute and her husband swears that she is insatiable. Voltore states that only today she enticed a stranger with her loose glances and even more lascivious kisses, and he alleges that Mosca saw them together in a gondola. Mosca speaks next and tells the court that a lady who saw them together and pursued them through the streets in order to save her husband's honour, is outside. The magistrates call for her and Mosca goes out to fetch her.

Commentary
Jonson's skill in plotting is very evident in this scene. The discovery by Bonario of Volpone's fraud and his action in informing the magistrates of it makes it seem that the game is up for Volpone at the beginning of the scene. However, this is a false dénouement, the real one only occurring at the very end of the play. We have seen Mosca manipulate the individual conspirators in previous scenes; here he orchestrates them *en masse*. There is a great deal of irony in the scene, particularly when the innocent Bonario is falsely accused by Voltore of the kind of deceit of which Volpone is guilty:

> So much more full of danger is his vice,
> That can beguile so, under shade of virtue. (61–2)

Jonson's view of the Law is not a flattering one, and we observe in this scene how easily the magistrates are swayed by the persuasive lying of Voltore and the false testimony of Corvino and Corbaccio.

There are many references to animals in this scene and the increase in the animal imagery indicates the debased nature of the accusers, rather than those they accuse. Corbaccio calls his son a string of animal names:

> Monster of men, swine, goat, wolf, parricide,
> Speak not, thou viper. (111–12)

Corvino refers to his wife's sexuality in animal terms and compares her to a 'partridge', a bird traditionally supposed to be lascivious, and says she 'Neighs like a jennet', a jennet being a small Spanish horse thought to be lecherous.

Ironically, when Bonario tells the truth about Mosca and Volpone at the beginning of the scene it carries less weight with the magistrates than the lies and perjury of the conspirators. He correctly describes both Mosca and his master:

His parasite,
His knave, his pandar. I beseech the court
He may be forced to come, that your grave eyes
May bear strong witness of his strange impostures. (15–18)

Bonario also identifies Voltore's unscrupulous nature:

I humbly crave there be no credit given
To this man's mercenary tongue. (94–5)

When Bonario is disclaimed and disinherited by his father he meekly accepts:

Sir, I will sit down,
And rather wish my innocence should suffer,
Than I resist the authority of a father. (112–14)

In this scene, and in the play as a whole, goodness is not enough, and is ineffectual against evil. Jonson is making a very ironical and oblique comment on the nature of the Law and the society it represents. The ability to plead eloquently in court, even to lie, carries more weight than the simple truth.

Act IV, Scene vi

Summary
Lady Would-Be enters and Mosca advises her to be resolute. She has never seen Celia before, and yet she immediately identifies her as the courtesan whom her husband has dallied with, and insults her. Having descended to vulgar abuse, Lady Would-Be hypocritically tries to excuse herself in the eyes of the court. In response to all the false allegations that have been made against them, the only defence that Celia and Bonario offer is to protest their innocence. At this point in the legal proceedings Volpone is brought in, still pretending to be totally infirm, and Voltore launches into a speech which states the truth, though by implication Voltore intends to signify the opposite of what he says: 'See, here, grave fathers, here's the ravisher'. He tries to get the maximum amount of effect from his speech by contrasting the accusations which have been made against Volpone by Celia and Bonario with Volpone's apparently weak appearance. Voltore continues in this vein, even asking whether Volpone should be tortured. Bonario replies that he would have him cross-examined. Voltore's final speech, accusing Celia and Bonario,

is an eloquent plea that slanderers should be punished, otherwise no one will be safe. The first magistrate gives the order for Celia and Bonario to be taken into custody, and for them to be kept apart: Volpone's silent appearance in court as an invalid has completely taken him in.

Mosca is jubilant at the verdict and congratulates Voltore, while reassuring Corvino that it was better for him that he should be known as a cuckold than as someone who was trying to prostitute his own wife. But Corvino still has his doubts about Voltore, which Mosca, as usual, manages to quieten. Corbaccio now comes in and asks Mosca to keep an eye on all of Volpone's possessions. Mosca reminds him that Voltore's fee must be deducted. Corbaccio offers two chequeens, but Mosca says this is not enough and suggests six. Corbaccio finally settles on three, which he gives to Mosca as well as something for himself. Mosca is amazed by his meanness. Lady Would-Be expresses a desire to see Volpone, but Mosca puts her off by telling her that he is going to get Volpone to place her first in his will. At the end of this scene it appears that the evil have triumphed over the innocent in a court of law.

Commentary
The last of the legacy hunters, Lady Would-Be, now makes her appearance in court, and proves herself as unscrupulous and as capable of perjury as the others. The violence of her verbal attack on Celia, in which she calls her many animal names, shows the coarse side of her nature:

> Out thou chameleon harlot! Now thine eyes
> Vie tears with the hyena . . . (2–4)

After this outburst she apologises to the court:

> Surely, I had no purpose
> To scandalise your honours, or my sex's. (7–8)

The irony lies in the fact that Lady Would-Be has no modesty and pretends to be modest, whereas Celia, who is modest, is falsely accused by her and says nothing. She also shows herself to be a hypocrite.

Jonson criticises the legal system through the exchange between Bonario and the magistrates in which they ask him to produce witnesses:

> 1st AVOCATORE (TO BONARIO) What witnesses have you,
> To make good your report?
> BONARIO Our consciences.

CELIA   And heaven, that never fails the innocent.
4th AVOCATORE   These are no testimonies.
BONARIO   Not in your courts,
Where multitude and clamour overcomes. (15–19)

It is hard to avoid the feeling that the playwright is drawing on his own experiences at the hands of the law in the court-room scenes. Accused of murder, then imprisoned, under threat of the death penalty until he could prove that he could read and write, branded on the thumb and released, also accused at different times of seditious writing and recusancy, Jonson is highly critical of what passes for justice in the courts. He is pointing out the difference between natural justice, real justice, and the judgements arrived at in the law courts. In the context of the play his implied moral judgement has been extended from the private into the public sphere. Previously the dramatist has satirised the individual greed of the fortune hunters, now he makes a criticism of the legal system which is supposed to represent the values of society and preserve the principles of justice. A grave miscarriage of justice then takes place, indicative of the reversal of normal values that Jonson presents in the play. Up to the very last scene of the play it seems that the law will punish the innocent and allow the guilty to go free.

Volpone's actual appearance in court is a silent one and Voltore makes a great deal of this in his pleas to the court. However, there is a great deal of dramatic irony intended by Jonson in his speeches and, without meaning to, Voltore touches on the truth about Volpone:

VOLTORE   See here, grave fathers, here's the ravisher,
The rider on men's wive's, the great impostor,
The grand voluptuary! (23–5)

At the end of the speech his rhetorical question reflects the truth: 'Perhaps he doth dissemble?' The effect of the irony in this speech would not be lost on the audience. The last three lines of Voltore's final summing-up, likewise, with great irony, indicate the overthrow of normal values which has taken place in the play, and could be applied more accurately to Voltore himself, and the others who have conspired in perjury and false accusations against the innocent:

VOLTORE   That vicious persons when they are hot and fleshed
In impious acts, their constancy abounds;
Damned deeds are done with greatest confidence. (51–3)

The theme of unnatural behaviour runs through the play, first coming to our attention in Volpone's unnatural family and conduct. Corbaccio's behaviour towards his son is consistently presented as unnatural. At the very beginning of the scene, before the magistrates have been swayed by the rhetoric of Voltore, the fourth magistrate states:

> The more unnatural part that of his father. (5)

Even Mosca comments on Corbaccio in similar terms when he is amazed by his stinginess in the payment to be made to Voltore for winning the case for them:

> MOSCA Bountiful bones! What horrid strange offence
> Did he commit 'gainst nature in his youth . . . (89–90)

All the play's characters, apart from Celia, Bonario and Peregrine exhibit a lack of common sense and balance which the playwright, by implication, considered necessary for the right conduct of life.

Act V, Scene i

Summary
The entire opening scene of the fifth act consists of a soliloquy from Volpone. He expresses his deep-felt relief at narrowly avoiding public exposure, and states that he was never unhappy with his disguise until now. He makes a contrast between the ease of private deception and the difficulties of the public deception which has taken place in court. Imaginary illnesses begin to plague him, he says that his left leg had started to have a cramp and he had felt himself struck by a fatal paralysis. He tries to be merry, to shake it off, and calls for a bowl of wine in order to put himself into a good mood. He drinks it off and says that any plot or ingenious knavery that will make him laugh heartily will restore him to his old self.

Commentary
It is possible to give a Freudian reading of the play. Freud's theory of the individual involves a triad: the unconscious, the ego and the superego. The unconscious, according to him, is created by the mechanism of repression. In this speech we witness an act of repression on the part of the main character, Volpone, in which he attempts to forget what is unpleasant and unthinkable, namely the fact of his own death. From a Freudian point of view this speech is the most significant one in the play, for in it Volpone's deepest fears, of old age, disease and the extinction of his ego in death begin to surface:

'Fore God, my left leg 'gan to have the cramp,
And I apprehended, straight, some power had struck me
With a dead palsy. Well, I must be merry,
And shake it off. (5–9)

Interestingly enough, Volpone himself has a psychosomatic view of illness, believing it to be caused by the mind:

A many of these fears
Would put me into some villainous disease,
Should they come thick upon me . . . (8–10)

Instead of dealing with his fears and coming to terms with them consciously, he decides to force them out and he uses alcohol to help him forget:

I'll prevent 'em
Give me a bowl of lusty wine, to fright
This humour from my heart. (*He drinks*) (10–12)

He then states that he will displace the fear with his old means of dealing with it:

Any device, now, of rare, ingenious knavery,
That would possess me with a violent laughter,
Would make me up again! (*Drinks again*) (14–16)

Volpone's imaginary illness is one of the central metaphors of the play. He adopts the strategy of sickness for a dual purpose; it enables him to fleece the legacy hunters, and by playing at being ill he allays his anxieties about the unthinkable – his own decline and death. Volpone's ceaseless quest for pleasure is like that of an immature individual who continually seeks pleasure and tries to avoid pain at all costs. Instead of confronting his anxiety, facing the fact of his own mortality and dealing with his fears rationally, Volpone tries to forget and repress the threat of the death of his ego, or self. He relieves his anxiety by drinking and indulging in his game of pretending to be sick. He forces his painful fears beneath the level of consciousness, repressing them. This scene is therefore remarkable in showing the psychological mechanism of repression at work.

Act V, Scene ii

Summary
Mosca seems less worried by their narrow escape than is his master, and mocks Volpone for his fears. He plumes himself on the

success of his scheming and Volpone praises them both and goes on to say that he is more delighted than if he had enjoyed Celia's favours. Mosca continues to praise himself, although he gives Volpone some credit too. It delights Mosca that they managed to fool the court, while Volpone gloats over the fact that they have made the innocent suffer. Volpone is tremendously amused, and also surprised, that Mosca has carried it off, so that the legacy hunters who were so divided among themselves did not suspect anything. Mosca replies that they are so full of hopes that they ignore anything which indicates the contrary.

Volpone mimics Voltore's words in court and mocks his presentation of the case. He says that he could hardly forbear from laughing, but Mosca, more accurately, says that he seemed to be sweating, and Volpone admits it. The parasite goes on to ridicule Voltore's efforts expressing the belief that he deserves to be cheated. Exultant with their success, Volpone now determines to vex all the legacy hunters, so he tells Nano and Castrone to give out the news that he has died of grief because of the slander that was laid against him. Initially, Mosca does not see the purpose of this and he asks Volpone what he means by it. Volpone explains that he will instantly have the predatory would-be heirs rushing to the house, 'Greedy and full of expectation'. Mosca imagines that Volpone will then dash their hopes by appearing alive, but Volpone has other plans. He proposes that Mosca should dress up in a nobleman's gown and behave as if he is Volpone's heir, and show them a will naming him as such.

Volpone tells Mosca to treat them shabbily. The servant, being more practical than his master, asks what he should do if they ask to see the body. Volpone tells him to say that it has gone rotten, and Mosca adds that he will say that it was stinking and that he had been forced to have it put in a coffin and sent away. Volpone readily agrees to this and also gives Mosca his will, and further instructs him that he should sit with a cap on his head, and an account book, pen ink and papers before him, as if he was making an inventory of Volpone's possessions. Volpone himself wants to sit behind the curtains on a stool so that he can listen, watch their reactions, and enjoy a good laugh.

Mosca says that the news will numb Voltore, and Corbaccio will curl up like a louse when it is touched, while Corvino will run mad through the streets the next day with a rope and dagger. When Mosca comes to Lady Would-Be, who appeared in court to bear false witness, Volpone interrupts to describe how she kissed him in court before all the judges, when his face was running with oil. Mosca reminds his master that his face was also running with sweat, and goes on to speak of the restorative power of gold. Mocking Lady Would-Be, Volpone says that he thinks she loves him, while Mosca adds that she is ardently amorous for him. There is knocking at the door and

Mosca says that it is Voltore – the vulture has the keenest scent. Volpone says that he will go to his hiding place, while Mosca must take up his agreed position. He tells Mosca to be a craftsman and torture them skilfully.

Commentary
This scene marks a shift in the relationship between Volpone and Mosca. Up to this point Mosca has constantly deferred to his patron, but now he mocks Volpone for his lack of courage in court. Volpone also shows a serious lack of judgement in placing too much trust in Mosca. He imagines that Mosca is totally faithful to him, but once named as heir, with Volpone supposed dead, Mosca will show that he has a mind and plans of his own. The other mistake made by Volpone is in underestimating Mosca who has already proved himself his equal in cunning and quick-wittedness, and superior to him in terms of sheer nerve.

At the beginning of the scene the two arch-deceivers are in a self-congratulatory mood:

> MOSCA   Here we must rest; this is our masterpiece;
> We cannot think to go beyond this. (13–14)

It is Volpone's desire to go even further that causes him to overreach himself and brings about his eventual downfall. Mosca has more practical good sense.

The callousness and cruelty of Volpone are fully revealed to the audience as he gloats over the fact that they have made the innocent suffer:

> And quite divert the torrent
> Upon the innocent. (17–18)

To play confidence tricks on the greedy and predatory is one thing; to delight in making the innocent suffer is another. Volpone loses any remaining shreds of sympathy from the audience at this point and from here to the end of the play he progresses inevitably towards his richly deserved downfall. His comment on the eagerness of the fortune hunters indicates the moral depths that his plotting has reached: 'Like a temptation of the devil'. Volpone also seems a prey to wishful thinking when he says that, in court, 'I had much ado to forbear laughing.' Mosca, who is a keener and more truthful observer, replies:

> MOSCA   'T seemed to me, you sweat sir.
> VOLPONE   In troth, I did a little. (37–8)

From this point on, it is clear that Mosca has a firmer grasp of the situation than Volpone himself, and when, through over-confidence, Volpone places himself in his power by giving out that he is dead, Mosca is more than willing to take advantage of it.

Act V, Scene iii

Summary
Drawn by the news of Volpone's death, Voltore enters his house where Mosca is busily counting the number of carpets. He erroneously believes that he has inherited everything, and that Mosca is making a list of Volpone's possessions for his benefit. Mosca carries on making his list and, when Voltore asks to see the will, ignores him. Corbaccio enters next, brought by the news that has brought Voltore, but Mosca ignores them both, and continues counting. When Corvino arrives Volpone peeps out from his hiding-place to observe them. Corvino wonders why Voltore and Corbaccio are there. With the entry of Lady Would-Be all the greedy prospective heirs are gathered. Corvino in turn demands the will from Mosca, in order to get rid of the others and, having kept them in suspense for as long as possible, Mosca finally breaks off from making his inventory and hands it over. Volpone observes all this from his hiding-place and notes how their eyes greedily search the will to find out what they have been left.

Voltore dashes all their hopes when he cries out 'Mosca is the heir!' Corbaccio, who is deaf, asks, 'What's that?' From his place of concealment Volpone observes and comments on their reactions. He describes how Voltore has been struck dumb, Corvino faints, Lady Would-Be is going to swoon and Corbaccio, alone, because of his deafness, still believes himself to be the heir. Corvino wonders if Mosca is being serious, and Mosca tells him that he is very busy and continues listing Volpone's possessions, in order to annoy them still further. He informs them, 'Tomorrow, or next day, I shall be at leisure to talk to you all.' This exasperates them even more and Corvino asks if this is the only outcome of his great expectations, while Lady Would-Be bluntly states, 'Sir, I must have a fairer answer.' Mosca replies that she shall, and tells her to leave his house; he also reminds her that she had offered herself to him if he would get her named in the will. Mosca uses their offers to him against them, now that they believe him to be Volpone's heir. He says to Corvino that he is a declared cuckold, but that he will not betray his offering Celia to Volpone, and tells him to go home. Corbaccio at last has discovered that he has been outwitted by Mosca and says, 'I'm cozened, cheated by a parasite slave.' Mosca orders him to be quiet and reminds him of his greed and his attempt to hire him to poison

Volpone. He also reminds him that he has openly declared in court that he has disinherited his son, and has perjured himself. He warns him that if he so much as utters a syllable he will reveal everything. Mosca has thus cunningly blackmailed all the suitors into silence, apart from Voltore, by threatening to make public what they have done.

Voltore still cannot accept what has happened and he remains behind, believing that Mosca has been doing everything for him, in order to get rid of the others: 'Nay, leave off now, they are gone.' Mosca proceeds to put him in his place, and rubs in the defeat of his expectations still further by pretending to be sorry for disappointing him. He informs him that he almost wishes that he was not the heir, but he says the wishes of the dead must be respected, and goes on to tell him that he has a gift, thanks to his education, and 'while there are men,/And malice to breed causes' he will never want. (Jonson is having another dig at lawyers here.) To add insult to injury he says that he will pay Voltore the usual fee, and to further rub it in, he thanks him for his gift of plate. His final barbed comment to Voltore is to tell him that he looks constipated and had better go home to purge himself. At this Voltore leaves.

Now that the last of the legacy hunters has departed, Volpone comes out of his hiding-place and orders Mosca to put on his nobleman's gown and parade through the streets, in order to torment the disappointed heirs still further. He wishes that he could think of some disguise in which to meet them and to ask them questions, to further annoy them. Mosca replies that he can manage it, since he knows one of the officers of the court who resembles Volpone. He will go straight away, make him drunk, and bring Volpone his uniform. His master thinks that this is a rare disguise and one befitting Mosca's cleverness. Mosca warns him that they will curse him, but Volpone replies, 'The Fox fares ever best when he is cursed.'

Commentary
Volpone enjoys being a spectator of the behaviour of his would-be heirs at the news of his death, and their reaction to the revelation that they have been outwitted. There is something of the sense of a play within a play in this scene, with Mosca playing to the full his role of heir, and Volpone observing from his concealed vantage-point. The delight that they both take in the tormenting of the fortune hunters shows the sadistic sides of their natures. Mosca and Volpone, having revealed the greed in their victims and exploited it ruthlessly to gain favours, now destroy their hopes completely. The audience would have a sense of poetic justice at this. It also allows Mosca the opportunity to tell them exactly what he thinks of them. The one surprise for the audience is that Lady Would-Be has actually offered

herself to Mosca, in order to be mentioned in the will. The irony lies in the fact that she has come to Venice to study the habits of the Venetian courtesans and has ended up, just like them, selling herself for money. The audience would be expected to contrast her behaviour with that of Celia, who refused to sleep with Volpone despite all his offers to her. Jonson purposely counterpoints and contrasts his two female characters.

Mosca reserves his most acrimonious abuse for Corbaccio, whose meanness he detests:

> MOSCA   Yes, sir. Stop your mouth,
> Or I shall draw the only tooth, is left.
> Are not you he, that filthy covetous wretch
> With the three legs, that here, in hope of prey,
> Have, any time this three year, snuffed about
> With your most grov'ling nose; and would have hired
> Me to the pois'ning of my patron? Sir? (65–71)

Once again Jonson shows his remarkable talent for invective in Mosca's vituperative comments.

This confrontation between Mosca and the legacy hunters is the comic high point of the play. Volpone's commentary on the action from his position of concealment also indicates to the actors how they should react to the news:

> VOLPONE   (*Aside*) My advocate is dumb, I look to my merchant,
> He has heard of some strange storm, a ship is lost,
> He faints: my lady will swoon. Old glazen-eyes,
> He hath not reached his despair, yet. (23–6)

Here, as throughout the play, Jonson uses the aside as a dramatic device for commenting on the action.

The scene has shown a complete reversal in the hopes of the fortune hunters and, to add to their discomfiture, Mosca roundly abuses them. The groundwork for this comic *tour de force* has been laid in the preceding four acts, and Jonson's masterly development and climax to the comedy of the situation make this the funniest scene of the play.

Act V, Scene iv

Summary
The action switches to the sub-plot, involving Peregrine and Sir Politic Would-Be, and is set in Sir Politic's house. Peregrine enters disguised as a merchant, together with three real merchants, whom

he informs that he only wants to scare Sir Politic; then the others leave. When the waiting woman enters, Peregrine asks her to let her master know that a merchant on urgent business wishes to speak to him. Sir Politic replies, through the woman, that he is busy with weighty affairs of state and tells him to come some other time. Peregrine asks jokingly whether the grave affairs of state are how to make Bologna sausages without one of the ingredients, and eventually Sir Politic puts in an appearance. It transpires that the weighty affairs of state are the disagreement that has arisen between the knight and his wife. Sir Politic tells Peregrine that he has been writing an apology to her.

Peregrine apologises for bringing him even worse news, but the gentleman he met yesterday (Peregrine himself) is a spy, who has told the Senate that Sir Politic has a plot to sell the state of Venice to the Turks. Warrants have been signed for his arrest and for the searching of his study for papers. Sir Politic declares that he has nothing but notes taken from books of plays. Terrified, he asks Peregrine what he should do, and Peregrine advises him to hide himself in a sugar chest or basket, and he will send him aboard a ship. Sir Politic adds that he only spoke to the man as he did for the sake of conversation. There is knocking outside, Peregrine warns him that the arresting officers have come, and this puts Sir Politic into a panic. Peregrine asks the knight if he has a currant barrel to jump into and advises him to hurry because they will put him on the rack. In reply Sir Politic assures him that he does have such a device. Just then the merchants begin to call his name off-stage. Sir Politic avers that he will never endure torture and he lets it out that his device for hiding is a tortoise-shell designed for such emergencies. He asks Peregrine to put it on him, saying that, with a cap on his head and black gloves for his hands, he will pretend to be a tortoise until the officers have gone, and he orders his wife's women to burn his papers.

Peregrine goes out and the merchants rush in, demanding to know where Sir Politic is hidden. One asks where his study is, and at this point Peregrine re-enters, saying that he is a merchant come to look at the tortoise. When the first merchant enquires what kind of beast it is, Peregrine replies that it is a fish, and goes on to tell them that they can strike it and tread upon it. The merchants proceed to torment Sir Politic in his disguise, prodding him with a sword. Eventually they pull off the shell and discover him, whereupon Peregrine removes his own disguise and informs Sir Politic that they are even. Peregrine's last words to Sir Politic are: 'Farewell most politic tortoise.'

Peregrine has humiliated Sir Politic in public and his illusion of himself as a wise and experienced traveller is shattered. The ease with which Peregrine has duped him has revealed his credulity to himself, and Sir Politic indicates his fears that he has become a public laughing-stock. The servant woman announces that Lady Would-Be has returned home very depressed (because of the failure of her scheme to benefit from Volpone's will.) She has determined to go straight to sea as a cure, and Sir Politic declares his intention to leave Venice for ever and to be more sensible in future.

Commentary

Jonson increases the audience's interest by moving the action to the sub-plot. The main plot has reached a kind of climax and this is the final, climactic scene of the sub-plot, in which Peregrine teaches Sir Politic a lesson, as he announces to the merchants when he says, 'All my ambition is to fright him only.' As suggested previously, the sub-plot imitates the main plot in many respects, but there are important differences. In the main plot Volpone disguises himself as a sick man in order to cheat and defraud the legacy hunters; in the sub-plot Peregrine disguises himself as a merchant in order to frighten Sir Politic and bring him to his senses. Volpone's activities are for the purpose of cheating people: Peregrine's are for Sir Politic's ultimate good.

In the exchange between Peregrine and the merchants, Jonson makes it plain that he is again satirising both the craze for foreign travel and the many travel books that appeared at the time. The Englishman abroad has been a traditional subject for satire from Nashe's *The Unfortunate Traveller* to Kingsley Amis's *One Fat Englishman*, and there are echoes of Nashe's book in *Volpone*. Some critics have claimed that Jonson is satirising an actual historical person in the character of Sir Politic and is poking fun at Sir Henry Wotton who was the English ambassador to Venice at the time. Travel abroad, later known as the Grand Tour, was considered part of the education of the aristocratic Englishman, and Jonson himself undertook a trip to France in 1612 as mentor to Sir Walter Raleigh's son, six years after the first performance of *Volpone*.

Ben Jonson used the comic possibilities of the Englishman in foreign parts to the full. In the sub-plot he satirises both the idiosyncrasies of Sir Politic and his peculiar opinions of the Venetians, as well as the whole genre of travel writing:

> PEREGRINE   Yes, and ha' his
> Adventures put i' th' *Book of Voyages*,
> And his gulled story registered for truth? (4–6)

Peregrine is referring to Hakluyt's *The Principal Navigations, Voyages, Traffics and Discoveries of the English Nation*, published 1598–1600, an account of the voyages of discovery and exploration undertaken by Englishmen of the time. The period was one of great expansion of trade and increased exploration and colonisation, some of which Jonson mocks in Sir Politic's fanciful schemes for making money through trade. Jonson is also glancing at the unquestioning credulity of the readers of such works, as well as the gullibility of Sir Politic Would-Be himself.

Jonson extracts much humour from the pretentious absurdities of Sir Politic, foibles which cause the servant to go back and forth between Peregrine and her master. In the first instance he refuses to speak to Peregrine because he says he has 'weighty affairs of state', and secondly because Peregrine uses the word 'tidings', which shows that he is no statesman. Finally, when he does appear, Peregrine learns that the weighty affairs of state are the dispute that has broken out between Sir Politic and Lady Would-Be over Mosca's false accusation. Sir Politic is also prone to paranoia and suspects plots against himself, so that when Peregrine tells him that the gentleman he met yesterday (Peregrine himself) is a spy, he immediately believes it. Peregrine has made a correct assessment of his weaknesses and faults, and uses them against him, to persuade him to make a fool of himself. His credulity, in particular, makes him fall victim to the practical joke that is played on him.

Sir Politic is also extremely fearful and of a nervous disposition, so that when Peregrine mentions warrants to arrest him and to search his study, plus the possibility of torture, he readily agrees to hide himself. When, in response to Peregrine's enquiry as to whether he has a sugar chest, Sir Politic improves on this by suggesting that he hide himself in a tortoise-shell, he lays himself open to further ridicule. Most of this scene is pure farce, with Sir Politic appearing more ridiculous by the minute, and this must inevitably lighten the mood of the audience after the more serious tone and implications of the main plot.

Just as Volpone and Mosca torment the legacy hunters in the main plot, so Peregrine and the merchants tease Sir Politic in his ridiculous disguise. They prick him with their swords, order him to creep, and finally lift off the shell and reveal him. It is no accident that the playwright chose the tortoise for Sir Politic's disguise, as it is known for its timidity and ability to hide within its shell. Sir Politic's final words indicate this appropriateness:

> SIR POLITIC And I, to shun this place and clime for ever,
> Creeping, with house on back; and think it well,
> To shrink my poor head in my politic shell. (87–9)

Peregrine's humiliation of Sir Politic in public has had a beneficial effect on him. His illusions about himself have been shattered and he has gained a deeper understanding and increased self-knowledge, so that in future he will behave more prudently. In addition Jonson's choice of tortoise to symbolise Sir Politic's new found wisdom relates to his ingenious use of animal imagery and symbolism in the play.

Act V, Scene v

Summary
Volpone enters his house dressed as an officer, in the company of
Mosca, who is wearing the clothes of a gentleman. Volpone asks
Mosca if he resembles the court officer he is impersonating, and
Mosca says that no one could tell them apart. When Mosca enquires
what he is supposed to be, Volpone replies that he is a Venetian
nobleman, and scathingly adds that it is a pity he was not born one.
Mosca's retort to this is that, if he can hold on to the position he has
been given, all will be well, indicating that he is already planning
ahead, and will not readily give up his new status. Volpone ignores
this, however, as he is too busy looking forward to escaping from his
enforced confinement, and going out to see what news there is at the
court.

When Volpone leaves, Mosca reveals that he will force Volpone to
come to an agreement with him before he allows him to resume his
own identity. Mosca first lets Androgyno, Castrone and Nano go out
to play. It soon transpires that this is not the benevolent act which at
first it seems: Mosca wants them out of the way so that he can carry
on with his schemes uninterrupted. Mosca is triumphant; he now has
the keys, and possesses everything. He is Volpone's heir and will
remain so unless Volpone gives him half of his wealth. If he cheats
Volpone of everything, no one will blame him for it; it is the price of
Volpone's entertainment. Ominously he says, 'This is called the
Fox-trap.'

Commentary
Mosca is painfully aware of his humble origins. In an earlier scene
with Bonario, in III.ii, he refers to his being obliged to work as a
servant because he was not born heir to a fortune, and in this scene
Volpone mocks him to his face for his lowly birth:

> 'Fore heaven, a brave clarissimo, thou becom'st it
> Pity thou wert not born one. (4–5)

If there is any justification for Mosca's evil actions, it is to be found in
his wish to rise above his humble beginnings, and a desire to revenge
himself on a world which has treated him harshly. Volpone's contempt for him, which he shows openly here, is one of the possible
justifications for the course of action he is about to take against his
master.

The period that Ben Jonson was living in was one of rapid
economic and social change, and upward social mobility was possible,
because of the decline of feudalism. There was therefore great
concern for gaining social position. Shakespeare's father wished to be

considered a gentleman, and ordered his own coat of arms. Ben Jonson was frequently reminded of the fact that he had been a bricklayer by other playwrights who were envious of his writing talent and his success. Mosca's wish for respectability and status would not have been considered an ignoble one at the time, certainly not by Jonson himself, who came from an artisan background. It is the methods which he stoops to, his occupation of parasite, and his complete lack of conscience and moral sense which the audience must find reprehensible. Mosca'a consciousness of his low social position helps to explain his readiness to do anything to rise in the world, and it helps to make him a more fully developed character. Jonson's drawing of his characters in *Volpone* is very far from the simple, one-dimensational humour type of characterisation, described by some critics of the play. Mosca is one of Jonson's most believable and successful creations, and he dominates both his master and the play, retaining a firm hold on the audience's imagination. Volpone is not aware of his parasite's social ambitions, or if he is, mocks them and considers them of no importance. Volpone seriously underestimates Mosca, even though Mosca gives him a hint in this scene of what he is planning to do, when he replies to Volpone's gibe at his low beginnings with the following words:

> If I hold
> My made one, 'twill be well. (4)

But Volpone pays no attention to this: he is too busy looking forward to his excursion in disguise. Volpone is eager to escape from the restriction of his movements to the house caused by the need to convince the suitors that he is ill. Now that they believe him to be dead, he is able to go about freely and annoy them as he wishes.

When Volpone leaves the stage Mosca unfolds his real plans. He has no love for his master, and determines to make the most of the situation that has placed Volpone in his power. In the first place, he is determined to make him suffer in his disguise, unless he comes to an agreement.

> Do so. My Fox
> Is out on his hole, and ere he shall re-enter,
> I'll make him languish in his borrowed case,
> Except he come to composition with me. (6–9)

Jonson here echoes the sub-plot, where Sir Politic has been made to suffer in his disguise of a tortoise. Secondly, Mosca is determined to force Volpone to give him half of his wealth:

> So, now I have the keys, and am possessed.
> Since he will needs be dead afore his time.

> I'll bury him, or gain by him. I'm his heir,
> And so will keep me, till he share at least. (12–15)

Volpone's identification with the fox is made explicit in Mosca's comments, when he says, 'My Fox is out of his hole', and in his final ominous words: 'This is called the Fox-trap.'

Act V, Scene vi

Summary
Corbaccio and Corvino are in conversation outside the Scrutineo where the court is sitting. Corvino advises his fellow conspirators that they must stick to their first story for the good of their reputations. Corbaccio insists that his story is no invention, because his son would have killed him. Corvino agrees, and reminds Corbaccio of his will, which left everything to Volpone and which Mosca still has. Corbaccio tells him that he will demand it back from Mosca, now that Volpone is dead.

Volpone enters in his disguise as an officer of the court, greets them both, and wishes them joy for the sudden good fortune which has come to them from old Volpone. Corbaccio is furious and orders him away. Volpone continues to taunt them, reminds Corbaccio of how he changed his will, and then turns his attentions to Corvino. He tells him that he likes his spirit for not being too puffed up with his good fortune, and asks him whether Volpone gave him everything. Corvino tells him to go away, but Volpone stays and jeers at him for his wife's supposed unfaithfulness. He tells him that he should not worry, for he is rich enough to help him bear it, and even more so because of his luck, unless Corbaccio has a share. When Corbaccio orders him away, Volpone tells him he does not want to be acknowledged as the heir: it is wise to pretend; all gamblers do the same, at all games of chance, so that no one seems to win. This final taunt drives off Corbaccio and Corvino; then Volpone sees Voltore arriving, and prepares to torture him.

Commentary
Volpone's behaviour in this scene seems remarkably childish, but from another perspective he can be seen to be punishing the legacy hunters for their covetousness. His desire to torment them has placed him in Mosca's power, and will eventually lead to his downfall.

Act V, Scene vii

Summary
Voltore enters, reprimanding himself because he let a parasite outwit him. Volpone, still in disguise, tells him that the court is waiting for

him, and pretends that he thinks that Voltore is the real heir. He says
that he rejoices in his happiness, and that the money has fallen into
such learned hands, that understand how to handle it. He claims to be
a suitor, and asks Voltore for the small house in bad repair which is at
the end of his long row of houses by the fish market. He adds that it
was a popular brothel in Volpone's time, before he became diseased,
and the house and his body decayed at the same time. Voltore tells
him to shut up, but Volpone asks him to let him have first refusal. At
last Voltore understands that he is being mocked for his misfortune,
and goes off. Volpone sees Corvino and Corbaccio at the next corner,
and returns to annoy them further.

Commentary
In the play both Volpone and Venice are portrayed as decaying and
diseased:

> VOLPONE   . . . it was, in Volpone's time,
> Your predecessor, ere he grew diseased,
> A handsome, pretty, customed bawdy-house,
> As any was in Venice (none dispraised)
> But fell with him; his body, and that house
> Decayed together. (10–14)

A connection is established between Volpone and the brothel; in
addition there is the implied suggestion that Volpone died of veneral
disease. Venice was considered both corrupt and decadent, as well as
being famous for outbreaks of bubonic plague brought from the East.
This image of Venice persists to the present day: in Visconti's film
'Death in Venice', made in 1971, Venice was used as a symbol of
decadence and decay, with the plague raging in the background.

Act V, Scene viii

Summary
Corbaccio points out to Corvino that, like them, Mosca is wearing a
nobleman's gown, and this infuriates both of them. Volpone adds to
their anger by asking if what he has heard about the parasite is true.
Corbaccio is not pleased to see him again, but Volpone says that he is
sad that a wise old man like him should be got the better of. He adds
that he never could stand the parasite's hair, and thought that even
his nose seemed deceitful. There was something in his glance which
promised the ruin of a nobleman. He mocks Corvino, by telling him
that he thinks that one so experienced in the world, and a fine witty
merchant with such moral meanings in his name, should not have
sung his shame and dropped his cheese, to let the fox laugh at his
emptiness. In response to this Corvino threatens to beat him, despite
the privilege he has of wearing the uniform of a court official.

Volpone says that he is unwilling to stand up to the fury of a distracted cuckold and, as Mosca walks by, calls to him to save him. The others, unable to stand the sight of Mosca, leave. Volpone praises his parasite and tells him to turn upon Voltore.

Commentary
Volpone makes an explicit comparison between Corvino and the crow in the fable by Aesop, who drops the cheese when the fox tells him that he admires his singing. Corvino means 'crow' in Italian, while Volpone means 'fox'. Some critics have claimed that the original inspiration for *Volpone* was such bird and beast fables:

> . . . Corvino,
> That have such moral emblems on your name,
> Should not have sung your shame, and dropped your cheese,
> To let the fox laugh at your emptiness. (11–13)

Volpone makes the taunting comparison more direct by reminding Corvino of how he admitted he was a cuckold in court: 'Should not have sung your shame'. In this instance Jonson has fitted the events of the play very closely to the fable, and the animal allegory behind the play is referred to directly. This adds another level of meaning, but here, as elsewhere, the playwright's touch is light and he does not overdraw the analogy.

Act V, Scene ix

Summary
Voltore enters and insults Mosca, calling him a flesh-fly, and warns him that although it is summer with him now, winter will come. Mosca's reply is to ask him not to use abusive language, nor to threaten him. He advises him to get a bigger lawyer's hat because his brain is breaking loose, and exits. Volpone reappears, addresses Voltore, and offers to beat Mosca and throw dirt upon his first good clothes. Voltore makes a remark which shows that he realises that Volpone and Mosca are acting together. Volpone reminds him that the court is waiting for him. He also pretends to be incensed that a mule (Mosca), who has never read Roman Law, should get the better of an advocate. He continues to annoy Voltore by asking him why he did not have some legal ploy to avoid being tricked by such a creature, and hopes that Voltore is only joking, and that Mosca has not managed to do so. He remarks that it is only a conspiracy between Voltore and Mosca to fool the others, and Voltore is really the heir. Volpone's words hit their mark and Voltore is enraged. Delighted at Voltore's reaction, Volpone asks again how could it be

that he should be so cheated: what man could be clever enough to do it, as he is so wise and prudent? It is fitting that wealth and wisdom should go together.

Commentary

> VOLTORE Well flesh-fly, it is summer with you now;
> Your winter will come on. (1–2)

In addressing Mosca in this way Voltore reminds us that the parasite's name means 'fly' in Italian. He is thus categorised with the legacy hunters, whose names of vulture, crow, and raven, also suggest that they feed on dead and putrefying flesh. The implications of calling someone a fly are even worse, for the fly is even less choosy about what it eats, and would be considered much lower than the other feeders on carrion.

Act V, Scene x

Summary
The scene moves to the court-room where the magistrates, notaries, and officers of the court enter, together with Bonario, Celia, Corbaccio and Corvino. Bonario and Celia are brought forward to be sentenced. Voltore speaks to the magistrates, and asks for their mercy to triumph once more over their justice, and calls on them to forgive. He says that he is distracted, and does not know whom to address first – the magistrates, or the innocents whom he has abused for most covetous ends. Corvino tells Corbaccio that Voltore is mad. Voltore goes on ignominiously to beg the pardon of the court. Celia praises heaven for its justice and Volpone berates himself for being caught in his own noose, while Corvino advises Corbaccio to be resolute, for nothing can help them now but brazening it out. Voltore tells the magistrate that he is not speaking out of madness, but only out of conscience, which now makes him tell the truth. He lays the blame for everything on Mosca and the first magistrate orders that he should be sent for. It is Volpone in his disguise as a court official who goes to fetch him.

Corvino tells the magistrates that Voltore is distracted because he hoped to be the heir of old Volpone who has just died, he himself has admitted as much just now. The magistrates ask whether Volpone is dead and Corvino replies that he has died since the court last met. The magistrate then asks Voltore whether Volpone was a deceiver, and Voltore replies that he was not: it was the parasite who deceived them. Corvino's response to this is to accuse Voltore of speaking out of mere envy because Mosca, the servant, got the legacy for which he hungered. Voltore asks the court to look at some papers which explain the truth. Corvino says that the devil has entered him. When they discover that Mosca is Volpone's heir the attitude of the magistrates immediately changes towards him. The third magistrate says that he is now a man of great fortune and the fourth magistrate sends the notary to entreat Mosca to come to the court, in order to clear up some doubts.

The second magistrate declares that the affair is like a maze, while the first one asks whether Corvino stands by his first report, to which his reply is that his position, his life, his reputation, are at stake. The first magistrate asks Corbaccio if his position is the same, and Corbaccio replies that Voltore is a knave with a forked tongue and so is the parasite. In reply to this Voltore begs the magistrates to read his notes. Finally, Corvino insists that they should believe nothing he has written, because Voltore is possessed.

Commentary

In this scene Voltore springs a complete surprise on his fellow conspirators – he decides to tell the truth. His motives for this change of heart are not particularly pure; despite going along with Mosca's fabrications against Celia and Bonario, and strenuously pursuing their conviction on false evidence, he has not benefited from Volpone's will. He is therefore bitter towards Mosca and is trying to revenge himself on him for completely deceiving him. He has nothing to lose when the truth comes out; as a lawyer he can say that the people he was acting for gave him incorrect information. Mosca's and Volpone's taunts at him for being outwitted have goaded him into seeking revenge. Both Volpone and Mosca have heaped insults on Voltore, not realising what a dangerous enemy he would become when he had nothing to lose:

> VOLTORE   It is not passion in me, reverend fathers,
> But only conscience, conscience, my good sires,
> That makes me now tell truth. That parasite,
> That knave, hath been the instrument of all. (16–19)

Voltore is still ignorant of the fact that Volpone and Mosca have been in league with each other in the confidence trick they have worked on the legacy hunters, and he attributes all the blame to Mosca.

Corvino's response is to seize on Voltore's statement that he is distracted and to impute his sudden change of heart to madness brought on by failing to become Volpone's heir. He adds that Voltore speaks out of mere envy because Mosca got what he longed for:

> CORVINO   He doth speak
> Out of mere envy, 'cause the servant's made
> The thing he gaped for; please your fatherhoods,

> This is the truth; though I'll not justify
> The other, but he may be some-deal faulty.
> VOLTORE   Ay, to your hopes, as well as mine Corvino
> . . . (27–31)

At this point in the play Voltore points out that Mosca has been fooling them both, a fact which still eludes Corvino.

Even the magistrates are shown in this scene as being unduly influenced by money. Jonson ironically points out the immediate power of money to change their view of Mosca:

> 4th AVOCATORE   Him that they call the parasite.
> 3rd AVOCATORE   'Tis true;
> He is a man of great estate now left.
> 4th AVOCATORE   Go you, and learn his name, and say the court
> Entreats his presence here, but to the clearing
> Of some few doubts. (38–41)

Public morality as exemplified by the law courts is as easily swayed by money as the private individual. Both private and public life in Venice are portrayed as corruptible. This scene is crucial to the action of the play, for it seems that Voltore is now going to tell the truth, which will lead to the discovery of Mosca's schemes and the freeing of Celia and Bonario. But it is only an added complication to the plot, so that when the final resolution comes, the audience will experience an even greater sense of relief.

Act V, Scene xi

Summary
The scene is set in the street. Volpone enters and in a short soliloquy begins to regret that he has so recklessly exposed himself to danger. He berates himself for creating a snare for his own neck and wilfully running into it for the sake of amusement, when he had just escaped and was free and clear. He remonstrates with himself for his stupidity when he thought of the scheme and Mosca seconded it. Mosca must now help him solve the problem or they will both be destroyed.

Nano, Androgyno and Castrone enter, and Volpone demands to know who let them out. He questions them as to where they are going and enquires whether they are going to buy gingerbread, or to drown kittens. Nano replies that Master Mosca told them to go outside and play, and took the keys. The news that Mosca has taken the keys further alarms Volpone, and he accuses himself again for being a fool because, instead of knowing when he was lucky, he indulged his whims and fancies. He orders his household to go and seek Mosca. He hopes that Mosca's purpose may be more honest than he fears. He asks them to bid Mosca to go straight to the court, where he will go and see if it is possible to make Voltore change his course of action by giving him new hopes. His mistake was to provoke the advocate.

Commentary
Volpone often reveals his innermost feelings to the audience in soliloquies. He now comes to the conclusion that he has overreached himself through his wilful desire to torment the unsuccessful legacy hunters, after he had wriggled out of the charges brought against him by Celia and Bonario. This is one of Volpone's rare moments of seriousness; he realises that he is now totally in Mosca's power, for only Mosca can save the situation.

In his meeting with his unnatural household in the street he belittles them:

> How now! who let you loose? Whither go you now?
> What, to buy ginger-bread, or to drown kitlings? (8–9)

Volpone, who has vast and insatiable desires, mocks them for their petty ones, and yet such is Jonson's attention to detail in the play that the desires Volpone attributes to his eunuch, hermaphrodite and dwarf, are miniature versions of his own. Gingerbread in Jonson's time was made in fantastic shapes and would have been covered in gilt, thus suggesting Volpone's desire for gold, while drowning kittens suggests the malice and spitefulness that motivates Volpone, only on a smaller scale. He thus unintentionally makes an ironic comment on his own activities.

It seems that Volpone normally keeps his freakish household confined indoors and is surprised to find them wandering in the street. The fact that they call Mosca 'master Mosca' does not go unnoticed by Volpone, who makes mock of the phrase by repeating it. This style of address suggests Mosca's new-found sense of power and importance now that he is presumed to be Volpone's heir. With his discovery that Mosca has taken the keys, Volpone's alarm increases and, for the first time, he realises how dependent he has made himself on Mosca. The last line of the scene indicates that Volpone now realises that enraging Voltore has been his undoing:

> When I provoked him, then I lost myself. (22)

Act V, Scene xii

Summary
The final scene of the play is set in the Scrutineo where the magistrates, Voltore, Bonario, Celia, Corbaccio, Corvino and officers of the court are gathered. The first magistrate indicates Voltore's papers and says that his various statements are inconsistent. Voltore has admitted that Bonario has been wronged and that Celia was compelled by her husband to go to Volpone and was left there. Voltore states that this is so. The first magistrate goes on to say that, on the other hand, Voltore believes the allegation against Volpone – that he attempted to rape Celia – to be false, because he knows that he is impotent. Corvino interrupts at this point and insists that Voltore is possessed and mad.

Volpone, in his disguise as an officer of the court, enters and announces, 'The parasite will straight here, grave fathers.' He is immediately reprimanded by the fourth advocate who tells him that he should call Mosca by another name and says that when he arrives everything will be cleared up. Voltore has just begun speaking to the magistrates, when he is interrupted by Volpone, who whispers to him that Mosca wants him to be informed of the following: that his master lives, that he is still the heir, that his hopes are still the same, and that this was only a joke to test him to see how he would behave.

Voltore asks him if he is sure that he is alive and Volpone replies ironically, 'Do I live sir?' Voltore now regrets that he was too unrestrained and Volpone assures him that he can make amends for it. They have said in court that he is possessed; he must fall down and appear so, and he himself will help to make it convincing. When Voltore falls down he tells him what to do to appear possessed.

Volpone announces that Voltore is recovering and he asks, 'Where am I?'. Volpone tells him to take heart because the worst is past, and he is free from demonic possession. The magistrates are taken in by his performance and Corvino adds that Voltore has often been subject to these fits. The first magistrate shows him his deposition to the court and asks him if he recognises it. Volpone tells him, in an aside, to disown it. Voltore says that he recognises the handwriting, but all that it contains is false. Bonario cries out that this is all trickery, and the second magistrate exclaims what a maze the affair is. The first magistrate now cross-examines Voltore and asks him whether Mosca is guilty; in reply Voltore states that he is no more guilty than his patron Volpone. The fourth magistrate demands to know whether Volpone is dead and Voltore now maintains that he is alive. On hearing this the second magistrate reminds him that he had said that he was dead, but Voltore denies it. The third magistrate interrogates Corvino and insists that he said so, but Corvino's reply is that he heard so.

At this point in the proceedings Mosca enters, and the magistrates treat him respectfully. The fourth magistrate says that if Volpone was dead he would bestow his daughter's hand in marriage on him. In an aside, Volpone tells Mosca that he was almost lost because Voltore had revealed everything, but now it is alright and he begs Mosca to say that he is alive. Mosca pretends to the court that he does not know him, and tells the magistrates that he would have come sooner, but that he was making the funeral arrangements for his patron, whom he intends to bury like a gentleman. On hearing this, Volpone says, again in an aside, that he is trying to bury him alive and to cheat him out of everything.

The fourth magistrate now says aside, that it is a match between Mosca and his daughter. In a low voice Mosca asks Volpone whether he will give him half his wealth, and Volpone replies that he will be hanged first. Mosca advises him to speak more softly. The first magistrate questions Voltore as to whether or not he affirmed that Volpone was alive. Volpone himself replies that he is, that Mosca told him so, and in another aside now tells Mosca that he will have half. Despite this offer Mosca still pretends that he does not know Volpone and wonders aloud who the drunkard is, demanding that anyone who knows him should speak up, for he has never seen his face before. Then, so that only Volpone can hear, he informs him that he cannot give it to him so cheaply now. The first magistrate asks Voltore what he has to say in response to Mosca's statement. Voltore replies that the officer of the court (Volpone in disguise) told him that Volpone was alive. Volpone himself now asserts that he did, and will maintain with his own life that he lives: Mosca told him so. Mosca himself addresses the magistrates and tells them that if such insolence as this is permitted against him, he will remain silent. He also expresses the hope that it was not for this that he was summoned to the court.

The second magistrate immediately orders that Volpone should be taken away and whipped, and taught to show respect for someone of Mosca's rank. In a last vain attempt to change his mind Volpone appeals to Mosca in an aside. The fourth magistrate orders Volpone away and he is seized; Mosca thanks the magistrate for this. Volpone now realises that he has nothing further to lose. He will be whipped and Mosca has taken possession of everything he owns; even if he confesses he cannot be punished much more. The fourth magistrate, now certain that Volpone is dead, asks Mosca if he is married. Volpone, alarmed, says aloud that he and Mosca will be allies through marriage soon, and he himself must be resolute. He puts off his disguise, saying, 'The fox shall here uncase.' Mosca is surprised by Volpone's act but, keeping his wits about him, pretends to reproach him for it. However this is to no avail for Volpone informs him that he will not be ruined alone; he will certainly prevent the marriage so that Mosca will not be able to use his wealth to worm his way into a good family. Volpone at last identifies himself to the court, and in his determination to make as many people suffer with him as possible, names all the other conspirators who have tried to mislead the court.

The magistrates realise that the complicated affair has been resolved, and order that Bonario and Celia, who are innocent, should be released. The first magistrate commands that Mosca should be stripped of his gentleman's gown. Corvino, Mosca and Voltore now beg the mercy of the court, but the response is harsh for they are told to stand forth for sentencing. Mosca is dealt with first, and is told that he appears to have been the ringleader in all these deceptions. He has also abused the court and the dress of a Venetian nobleman, by wearing it when he is a fellow of low birth. He is sentenced to be whipped and then to spend the rest of his life as a galley-slave. Volpone thanks them for this. Now it is Volpone's turn, and his sentence is that all his property should be confiscated and given to the Hospital of the Incurables and since he has gained so much from pretending to be lame and to be suffering from gout, palsy, and other diseases, he will be confined in shackles until he is sick and lame indeed. Volpone himself realises the justice of this when he addresses his final words to the court: 'This is called mortifying of a fox.'

Because of the scandal he has brought to his profession, Voltore is banished from the legal profession and from the state of Venice. Corbaccio is to be shut up for the rest of his life in the monastery of the Holy Spirit and his son Bonario is to be given his whole estate. Corvino is to be taken from his house and rowed around Venice, along the Grand Canal, wearing a cap with long ass's ears, instead of the horns of a cuckold, and to be placed in the pillory with a paper pinned to his breast giving details of his offences. To expiate the wrongs done to his wife Celia, he has to send her back to her father with her dowry trebled.

The first magistrate, who has pronounced sentence, tells them that now they will begin to think about their crimes. He orders them away, and asks that everyone who sees these vices so rewarded, should take heart and reflect on them. The final speech of the play belongs to Volpone, and is, in effect, a speech to bring down the final curtain. He asks for the audience's applause if he has not offended them.

Commentary
The final and climactic scene which resolves the action of the play

takes place in the courtroom. The sub-plot has already reached its conclusion with the departure of Sir Politic and Lady Would-Be from Venice. Sir Politic, who suffered from folly rather than vice, has learned his lesson, and leaves Venice a wiser man; in the main plot, however, the central characters exhibit serious vices, and the playwright feels that they have to be adequately punished. As Jonson notes in the prologue to *Every Man Out of His Humour*, where he places his own views in the mouth of his character Asper: ' . . . my strict hand was made to seize on vice'. Unlike the comedies of Aristophanes, which pre-dated the birth of Christ by four hundred years, and often ironically allowed evil to triumph, Jonson's play ends with an affirmation of Christian values, with the innocent being freed and the guilty punished. Jonson was in the position of many Renaissance classicists, who attempted to reconcile Ancient Greek art and thought with Christianity and, inevitably, in the last resort, came down in favour of Christian values.

Throughout the play there has been a total reversal of normal values: gold has been worshipped like a god, greed and avarice are triumphant, and the evil characters defeat the good. At the end of the play the traditional moral order is restored, and the innocent are freed, while the guilty are punished.

The scene opens in confusion, with the first magistrate unable to reconcile, or make sense of, the statements made by the various parties appearing in court. This confusion is caused by Voltore's attempt to get his revenge on Mosca, by telling the court what he imagines to be the truth, but which is in fact only partly the truth, because he does not realise that he has been deceived by Volpone all along. As previously mentioned Jonson is extremely fond of adding twists and turns to the plot.

Corvino insists that Voltore is mad, and yet, ironically, this charge could equally be made against all the principal characters, for their possession by the spirit of greed is the main subject of the play:

> CORVINO Grave fathers, he is possessed; again, I say,
> Possessed; nay if there be possession
> And obsession, he has both. (7–9)

The ineffectuality of conventional goodness in the corrupt world that is represented in the play is indicated by Celia's orthodox and pious platitudes, which bear little relation to what has happened to her. So far in the play she has been the victim of attempted rape, has been falsely accused of adultery in open court, and in addition has been wrongly imprisoned for attempted murder. Even at this juncture Voltore is only telling the truth because he wants revenge on Mosca – not because of any heavenly intervention, as his later retraction of his evidence shows. The audience is therefore forced to the conclusion that Jonson is being cynical about unthinking and uncritical Christian belief.

Jonson shows himself to be a master of comedy in this scene, as when Volpone, in his disguise as a court official, tries to let Voltore know that he is still alive and asks him, 'Do I live, sir?' There is also biting humour in the speed with which Voltore draws back from telling the truth, when influenced by his renewed greed and expectations of becoming Volpone's heir.

The details of diabolic possession which are supplied by Volpone and which allow the actor playing Voltore to indulge in buffoonery, are, in fact, based upon actual trials for witchcraft of the time, as the editors of *Ben Jonson's Works*, Herford and Simpson have shown. The author's use of this material through the impostor Volpone, and his tool Voltore, indicates Jonson's sceptical attitude toward such trials and the allied activity of casting out devils. When Voltore comes to himself, he utters for the first time in Western literature the immortal words: 'Where am I?' and Jonson's ability to make the audience laugh is again apparent. One of the lesser ironies of the play is that falsehoods are more readily accepted by the court than the plain truth, as when Voltore assures the court that all his statement is false, when in fact it is true. Further dramatic irony is added when Voltore answers the magistrate's question:

> 1st AVOCATORE   Is he not guilty then,
> Whom you there name the parasite?
> VOLTORE   Grave fathers,
> No more than his good patron, old Volpone. (44–5)

Only the audience knows that both Mosca and Volpone are the guilty parties. The readiness of the magistrates to change their opinions of the people appearing before them, and about the evidence presented to them, indicates Jonson's less than respectful, not to say derisive attitude towards lawyers. Throughout this scene irony is piled upon irony, as Voltore denies not only the fact of Volpone's death, but also that he ever said that he was dead. Jonson is as scathing towards public morality as represented by the magistrates as he has been towards private morality.

Mosca's growing independence of action becomes apparent in this scene. For the first time in the play he disobeys Volpone when he ignores his pleas to tell the court that he is alive. His hopes of gaining material advantage from the power he enjoys over Volpone surface when he demands half of Volpone's fortune to do this.

> MOSCA   Will you gi' me half?
> VOLPONE   First, I'll be hanged. (62–3)

The struggle between the two, equally motivated by greed, inevitably brings about the downfall of both. Mosca has made it apparent from early on in the play that he has scant respect for his master, considering himself his equal in cunning and superior to him in coolness and presence of mind. Now that he has Volpone in his power he is not going to let him off lightly. Their relationship is based on money, not on mutual respect. Stung by Volpone's refusal to let him have half of his wealth, Mosca seizes the chance to gain all of it. He therefore repudiates Volpone and pretends he does not recognise him.

> VOLPONE   (*Aside*) Soft, soft, Whipped?
> And lose all that I have? If I confess,
> It cannot be much more. (82–3)

The complete reversal of his fortunes brought about by his being outwitted by his parasite, losing everything he has to him and, in addition, the humiliation of a public whipping, is too much for Volpone, so he determines to get his own back on Mosca, even at the cost of exposing his own trickery.

> VOLPONE   The fox shall here uncase. (84)

Shortly afterwards Volpone reveals an additional motivation for his action:

> Nay, now
> My ruins shall not come alone; your match
> I'll hinder sure; my substance shall not glue you,
> Nor screw you, into a family. (85–7)

Volpone has made it plain in V.v that he considers Mosca to be his social inferior with his slighting remark that it is a pity he was not born a gentleman. The thought that Mosca should rise in society at the expense of his own fall is intolerable to Volpone, and is the final factor in his decision to identify himself to the court:

> VOLPONE   I am Volpone, and this (*Pointing to Mosca*) is my knave;
> This, (*To Voltore*) his own knave; this, (*to Corbaccio*)
> avarice's fool;
> This, (*to Corvino*) a chimera of wittol, fool, and knave . . . (88–91)

In thus revealing himself Volpone is determined to make as many people suffer with him as possible; he names all the other conspirators who have tried to mislead the court, as well as giving accurate thumb-nail sketches of their characters and vices.

When the first magistrate orders the release of Celia and Bonario, Bonario utters the somewhat unrealistic belief:

Heaven could not long let such gross crimes be hid. (98)

In fact the pious and conventional Christian morality of Celia and Bonario has been powerless before the cunning and duplicity of Volpone and Mosca and it is only when the two main conspirators fall out that the whole deception is revealed. The first magistrate makes a comment on the acquisitiveness of the guilty which could serve as a footnote to the play:

These possess wealth, as sick men possess fevers,
Which, trulier may be said to possess them. (101–2)

This is a fair description of the monomania presented in the play, and in particular that of Volpone, whose adoration of gold is his religion. In the final scene the major themes are made explicit.

The judgments handed down by the magistrates agree with the crimes of the guilty. Mosca's efforts throughout the play have been aimed at bettering himself at any cost, and his sentence is to be whipped and to spend his life as a galley slave, the lowest position in the Venetian state. Volpone's comment on this is 'I thank you for him.' Mosca's final words to Volpone are 'Bane to thy wolfish nature', which recalls the imagery of predatory animals so prevalent earlier in the play. Volpone's punishment is equally apt. Throughout the play he has pretended to be incurable in order to gain money from his victims, and the first part of his sentence is that his money should be given to the Hospital of the Incurables. The second part of his sentence is also extremely appropriate for one who has spent his time pretending to be sick:

And, since the most was gotten by imposture
By feigning lame, gout, palsy, and such diseases,
Thou art to lie in prison, cramped with irons,
Till thou be'st sick and lame indeed. Remove him. (121–4)

Volpone himself seems to realise the justice of this, when he addresses his final words to the court: 'This is called mortifying of a fox.' To the end he identifies himself with the animal whose name he bears. There is also a pun on the word 'mortifying', which could mean humiliating, or hanging game to make it tender, as well as putting to death. He compels our admiration with the final jest he makes as he accepts his fate.

The punishments of the other conspirators are likewise fitted to their crimes, and the first magistrate who has pronounced sentence makes a moral judgment on the activities which have been un covered:

> Let all see these vices rewarded,
> Take heart, and love to study 'em. Mischiefs feed
> Like beasts, till they be fat, and then they bleed. (149–51)

One of Jonson's purposes in the play has been to attack such vices as greed, lechery, pride and hypocrisy. The final summing up of the first magistrate also completes the imagery of feeding which runs throughout the play and is associated with the acquisition of wealth and with evil.

4 MEANING OF THE PLAY

Volpone can be read in many ways and on many levels. The text is complex and yields a variety of interpretations. Perhaps the most obvious reading of the play is as a satire. In his *Epistle* to *Volpone* Jonson stated that the function of a poet is 'to inform men in the best reason of living'. He attempts to do this by satirising various vices and follies: greed, credulity, hypocrisy, lust, gluttony, pretentiousness and pride. Volpone and Mosca are the agents through whom the avarice of their victims is aroused and exploited. As Volpone says in I.iv: 'What a rare punishment is avarice to itself,' to which Mosca's reply is, 'Ay, with our help sir.' Volpone himself is not above the dramatist's satire, however, for in his very first speech in the play Jonson ridicules his adoration of gold and, later, his lust for Celia.

By attacking human weaknesses satire implies certain standards and values: usually those of balance and moderation. Nowhere in the play does Jonson explicitly state or present the human qualities he prizes – he does it by implication. Celia and Bonario are not held up as models of behaviour, for their goodness is presented as ineffectual in the corrupt world of the play. The one example of a character who realises his foolishness and modifies his behaviour accordingly is Sir Politic Would-Be. He is brought to his senses and to a realisation of his folly by means of a practical joke. Presumably, Jonson hopes that by satirising vices and weaknesses, and by making his audience laugh at them, he will persuade it to shun such failings. Jonson's real plea is for man to rise above the animal, and to become more reasonable. The most serious vices in the play are given an animal form. The main object of Jonson's attack, greed, is allegorised by predatory animals, with the legacy hunters as birds of prey, and the central character as a fox. Like Aristophanes before him, Jonson believes that by caricaturing vice he will make mankind more virtuous.

But *Volpone* has other meanings and can be read in other ways. At the time that Jonson was writing there was a crisis of humanism in

England. The early optimistic note struck by Marlowe in his over-reaching heroes like Tamburlaine, had given way to a mood of scepticism shown by the growth of interest in writing satire, and Jonson's writing was part of this new mood. Like Marlowe's heroes, Volpone has enormous desires, but Jonson's attitude to them is critical. This turn of the century pessimism is indicated by such plays as *Hamlet*, with its hero's expression of profound disillusionment and despair at the human condition and his increasing preoccupation with thoughts of his own death and man's mortality. *Volpone* too, reflects this mood.

What is the deep meaning of the play? Beneath the surface comedy and satire the mood is one of extreme pessimism. If we look more closely at Volpone's actions they reveal a more profound meaning to the play. Volpone himself pretends to be dying in order to cheat the legacy hunters, but also to feel that he has conquered sickness, old age and death. The subtext of the play is the concern to cheat sickness and death and this frequently surfaces, even in scenes that are apparently comic, as when Volpone disguises himself as a mounte-bank who claims to be able to cure all illnesses and even to extend life. Humour is often our way of dealing with unpleasant truths or facts which threaten us, in this case our mortality. This is the human condition: man alone of the animals knows he will die.

The deep meaning of *Volpone* is man's fear of illness, old age, and death. In a sense *Volpone* is like *Everyman*, a medieval play in which Everyman, who literally represents every man, has to come to terms with his own death. The central speech of the play from this point of view is Volpone's speech in I.iv:

> So many cares, so many maladies,
> So many fears attending on old age,
> Yea, death so often called on, as no wish
> Can be more frequent with 'em. Their limbs faint,
> Their senses dull, their seeing, hearing, going,
> All dead before them; yea, their very teeth,
> Their instruments of eating, failing them –
> Yet this is reckoned life! . . . (144–51)

This fear returns to haunt Volpone in his soliloquy in V.i, when he imagines that he has been ill, and panic seizes him, until he drinks wine in an attempt to cheer himself up and to drive such thoughts from his mind:

> VOLPONE . . . Cavè, whilst I breathe.
> 'Fore God, my left leg 'gan to have the cramp,
> And I apprehended straight, some power had struck me

With a dread palsy. Well I must be merry,
And shake it off. A many of these fears
Would put me into some villainous disease,
Should they come thick upon me – I'll prevent 'em.
Give me a bowl of lusty wine, to fright
This humour from my heart (*He drinks*) Hum, hum, hum!
'Tis almost gone, already (4–13)

Volpone also declaims the importance of health when he appears disguised as Scoto of Mantua in II.ii:

O, health! health! the blessing of the rich! the riches of the poor!
Who can buy thee at too dear a rate, since there is no enjoying the world without thee? (87–90)

A connection is established between health and riches and Volpone, as Scoto, suggests that riches can buy health.

The ending of the play, which has puzzled many critics, who have considered Volpone's punishment too severe for his crimes, now assumes a new significance. Volpone's final punishment is to have the sickness and death which he has so far merely imitated, inflicted on him:

1st AVOCATORE   And since the most was gotten by imposture,
By feigning lame, gout, palsy, and such diseases,
Thou art to lie in prison, cramped with irons,
Till thou be'st sick and lame indeed. Remove him.
VOLPONE   This is called mortifying of a fox. (V.xii, 121–5)

Volpone's reply reveals that he has received a death sentence. As has been mentioned before, 'mortifying' has several meanings: to humiliate someone, to hang game until it is tender, and to kill someone. All these meanings are appropriate in the context, but the last one indicates that he has been sentenced to death. This gallows humour in his last speech to the court, the jest with which he acknowledges his sentence, forces us to admire the stoicism with which he faces death. Throughout the play Volpone has pretended to be dying in order to feel that he can cheat sickness and death. At the end of the play he is condemned to death, which he accepts. Thus the ending is emotionally satisfying.

The play also reflects the rise of capitalism and the decay of feudal and medieval values which occurred in the seventeenth century in England. Although Jonson is highly critical of the acquisition of wealth his comedies indicate the shift away from courtly values to middle-class ones. The majority of the characters in his comedies are from the urban middle class. Jonson's moral seriousness is typical of the rising Puritan values which superseded the aristocratic courtly ones. This ultimately led to the rejection of poetry for prose as the main vehicle of artistic utterance with the rise of the novel and the decline of the drama.

5 TECHNICAL FEATURES

5.1 CHARACTERISATION

Volpone

The names of many of the characters of *Volpone* are taken from Florio's Italian Dictionary *A Worlde of Words* which was published in 1598. These provide important clues for the audience. Volpone, for example, was defined as 'an old fox, an old reinard, an old craftie, slie, subtle companion, sneaking, lurking wily deceiver'. From his entrance in the first scene the audience is made aware that the dominating passion or 'humour' of Volpone is greed: his character is clearly revealed in the opening speech of the play. Jonson's characterisation is not to be faulted: psychology is familiar with people suffering from an *idée fixe* or an obsession. As Edmund Wilson has pointed out, the characters of both Volpone and his creator Ben Jonson fit comfortably into Freudian theory as anal erotic types. 'Such people, according to Freud, have an impulse to collect and accumulate . . . ' But we do not need to psychoanalyse either Ben Jonson or Volpone to realise that the basic impulse of the play's central character is pathological.

Volpone's natural human instincts have been transformed into an inordinate love of gold. He is childless and the mock family he creates around him is both unnatural and unhealthy. Volpone's character has been created by the displacement of natural instinct and its replacement with an unnatural one. Volpone sees love as a commodity which can be bought. When Mosca pleases him, he offers him money and in his attempted seduction of Celia he literally tries to purchase her. Gold has an artificial value placed on it because of its scarcity; because Volpone believes it to have real value, all his standards are artificial, and as gold is his highest good all his values are suspect.

But Volpone is no simple miser. He takes a delight in the pleasures of the senses which he describes in the speeches of seduction addressed to Celia. He also enjoys plotting and scheming and has contempt for those who merely hoard their wealth instead of enjoying it. Volpone suffers from a superabundance of desire, not only for material things, but also for Celia. He does not distinguish between the two. When Mosca tempts him in his description of Celia he says that she is 'Bright as your gold! and lovely as your gold!'

He goes to great lengths to prove that other people are as debased and materialistic as he is, beneath their hypocrisy and pretence. He wants to strip away the masks from people and reveal what lies underneath, and he uses the negative impulses of his victims to ensnare them: their materialism and their greed. In this sense he has almost a moral function: to reveal human hypocrisy and pretence.

Volpone is completely without conscience and fits into a long line of Machiavellian characters in Elizabethan and Jacobean plays. Despite this, he is easily the most fascinating character in the play and the audience identifies with him. There are several reasons for this. We are impressed by his energy, and Jonson also gives his speeches the most vivid imagery and the best poetry of the play. His delight in manipulating people and scheming also compels our attention. He has enormous desires which eventually lead him to overreach himself.

The audience cannot help identifying with him. In much the same way that an audience identifies itself with Punch in a Punch and Judy show, even though his antics, when considered coolly are morally reprehensible. Volpone has the same liberating effect on an audience, freeing it momentarily from its normal moral reservations. He invites our consciences to take a holiday. His relationship to his parasite Mosca is central to the play. Mosca both leads him on and expresses his desires.

Mosca

'Mosca' in Italian means 'fly' and as his name suggests he is the most degenerate character in the play. But even with him, Jonson provides some justification for his artfulness and mendacity. In several of his speeches Mosca reveals himself to be painfully conscious of his low birth and poverty, and we learn that all his efforts are directed at raising himself in the world. He reveals his character directly to the audience in his speech in praise of being a parasite in III.i. He suffers from pride and he delights in his own cleverness. This causes him to aim too high when he tries to outwit even Volpone and brings about the downfall of both of them.

Mosca is amoral and shows no finer feelings. In his dealings with the suitors and with Celia and Bonario he is totally ruthless and delights in the sufferings of others. He is also quick witted and capable of turning everything to his or Volpone's advantage. The audience feels no sorrow when Mosca receives his richly deserved punishment at the end of the play, whereas, for his master, some lingering sympathy remains. His name also suggests that he is an even lower form of scavenger than the fortune hunters, who are given the names of birds who feed on carrion. Finally, like the fly his namesake, he has a great capacity to annoy and irritate people, as when he torments the disappointed legacy hunters.

Voltore

His name was likewise taken by Jonson from Florio's dictionary. 'Voltore' is defined as 'a ravenous bird called a vulture'. Voltore's profession, that of lawyer, attracts Jonson's particular dislike. In several places Jonson mounts an attack on lawyers and their means of making a living. Voltore is avaricious, like the other legacy hunters, but at one point it seems that there is a spark of goodness in him when he informs the court that Celia and Bonario are innocent. This spark is swiftly extinguished by his greed. Through his greed he is manipulated by Mosca and Volpone, and he is largely responsible, through his persuasive tongue, for the court's initially finding Bonario and Celia guilty.

Corbaccio

'Corbaccio' means 'a filthie great raven' and like the other legacy hunters he is amazingly greedy. He is even prepared to disinherit his son Bonario and name Volpone his heir in order to benefit from Volpone's will. What is most striking about Corbaccio is that, as Volpone tells us in Act I scene iv, he is even more aged and infirm than Volpone himself, and yet hopes to outlive him. He is also hard of hearing, and Mosca uses this weakness to play jokes on him. Corbaccio is extremely gullible and is all too ready to believe ill of his son Bonario, who is innocent of the accusations made against him by Mosca. He is quite willing to murder Volpone in order to inherit his wealth, as when he offers Mosca a sleeping-draught for Volpone which is in fact poison.

Alone of all the legacy hunters he takes a particular delight in hearing of Volpone's supposed illnesses. His main motive in all this is his desire to outlive Volpone:

> Excellent, excellent, sure I shall outlast him:
> This makes me young again, a score of years. (I.iv. 55–6)

In many ways he is the most repellent of the predators and he attracts Mosca's particular hatred because of his extreme meanness. After the first trial of Celia and Bonario, when Voltore has won the plotters' case for them, he haggles with Mosca over Voltore's payment and reduces it by half.

Corvino

The merchant is the legacy hunter who is most deceived by Volpone. 'Corvo' means 'crooked, bent, hooked'; also 'a crow' and Volpone specifically refers to him when he mentions Aesop's fable concerning the fox and the crow, in I.ii. Despite his angry protests to Celia in II.v, that she has looked out of the window at the mountebank, he is prepared to prostitute her to Volpone in the hope of material gain. The irony lies in the fact that Volpone and the mountebank are one and the same person. Corvino, though apparently a jealous husband, places more importance on money than on his wife. This increases the audience's sense of his greed. In fact he is in such a hurry to offer Celia that Mosca remarks, 'Did e'er man haste so for his horns?'

His sense of honour is equally shallow. His jealous tirade at Celia began with the words: 'Death of mine honour with the city's fool', but by III.vii he tells her, 'Honour . . . a mere term invented to awe fools . . .' Jonson reveals his hypocrisy clearly and with great comic effect in such scenes. Because of his extreme gullibility he attracts some sympathy from the audience. In the court-room scene he falsely accuses Celia of having an affair with Bonario in order to escape being accused of offering her to Volpone himself. Thereby he offers himself up to public ridicule as a cuckold. Like Volpone, he values Celia as a commodity, not as a human being, as when he asks her, 'What is my gold the worse for touching?' when he is encouraging her to go to bed with Volpone. In addition to his greed, which is a characteristic shared by all the legacy hunters, Corvino also shows himself to be a hypocrite.

Lady Would-Be

Lady Would-Be is one of Jonson's great comic creations. One of her functions is to link the sub-plot with the main plot, as she is the only character, apart from Mosca, who appears in both; the other is to provide comic relief. She is garrulous, obsessed with her appearance, pretentious, superficial, a dilettante and a name-dropper. She reveals all these aspects of her character in her very first entrance in the play, when she visits Volpone. One of the lesser ironies in this scene is that she is the only one of the legacy hunters who inconveniences Volpone to the extent that he wants her to leave. He is maddened by her incessant chatter and begs Mosca:

> Rid me of this my torture quickly, there;
> My madam with the everlasting voice; (III.v. 3–4)

She reveals her meanness, in contrast with the generous presents of the other suitors, by giving Volpone a cap she has made. Her conversation darts from one topic to another without stopping for a moment. She is a poseuse, pretending to have knowledge about many subjects, but in fact her knowledge is shallow and trivial. Her chief concern is with her appearance. Jonson creates a great deal of comedy out of her ability to mangle the English language. Like Mrs Malaprop in Sheridan's *The Rivals*, she frequently uses the wrong word, merely because it is similar in sound to the one she intends, as for example when she says 'the golden mediocrity' instead of 'the golden mean', thus managing to convey the exact opposite of what she intends. It is possible that she suggested Mrs Malaprop to Sheridan.

Despite the fact that she offers herself to Mosca to be named in Volpone's will, she is extremely jealous and possessive with regard to her husband, and one of the great comic scenes of the play is where she mistakes Peregrine for a female prostitute dressed up as a man. She also believes in exposing as much of her body as possible, as appears in her speech to her maids in III.iv. In short, Lady Would-Be offers many splendid comic opportunities to the actress playing her part. She is the only one of the legacy hunters who moves the audience to laughter, rather than horror, at her activities.

Bonario

His name immediately suggests his character to the audience. Florio's definition has 'honest, good, uncorrupt'. In his first appearance his goodness and integrity are in total contrast to Mosca, and this is perhaps why Mosca wants to have him disinherited by his father. The meeting between the two in III.ii also indicates his gullibility when Mosca easily deceives him into believing that he is a good person. (Jonson seems to be saying that naive goodness is not enough.) He is defenceless before the kind of cunning and malevolent evil represented by Mosca. The fact that he manages to rescue Celia from Volpone's attempted rape is due to a slip of Mosca's – he misjudges Bonario's ability to overhear what is going on – rather than to any perception on Bonario's part. Even in the final scene of the play the exposing of the villainy of Volpone and Mosca is due to their falling out rather than to any action taken by Bonario. His purpose in the play is to suggest the standards by which the audience is to judge the activities of Volpone and Mosca.

Celia

Like Bonario she represents naive and ineffectual goodness. In her attempted seduction by Volpone the audience is struck by the simple language with which she replies to Volpone's colourful blandishments. Her responses are couched either in the idiom of conventional Christian belief of the time or in colourless language. Their two characters are diametrically opposed. She rates innocence as the highest form of wealth, whereas Volpone glories in the satisfaction of the senses. She represents Puritan self denial, Volpone aristocratic excess.

The representation of goodness on the stage is difficult. Innocence can appear pallid or uninteresting in comparison with evil and this is the case in the seduction scene. Volpone's energy and the vitality of the language he is given by Jonson appeal vastly more attractive to the audience than Celia's pious Christian platitudes. However, the emergence of Bonario from hiding immediately places events in perspective. Volpone offers no resistance to him whatsoever.

Celia is not a character to appeal to feminists for she is dependent on the actions of others. Celia is acted upon, rather than acting freely herself and is at the mercy of the male characters in the play. Her husband attempts to prostitute her to Volpone and her response is: 'Are heaven and saints then nothing?' Like Bonario she appears weak in contrast to the evil characters ranged against her. She is powerless before Volpone's attack, until Bonario appears from hiding to save her. In court, when false accusations are laid against her and Bonario, her only defence is to make an appeal to 'heaven that never fails the innocent'. One of her accusers is Lady Would-Be, and the contrast between Celia's modesty and Lady Would-Be's nasty nature is extremely marked. Jonson clearly intends us to make comparisons between them. Celia is inevitably linked in our minds with Bonario; together they represent normal standards in the distorted world of *Volpone*, and at the end of the play, after a period of confusion, it is these standards which triumph.

Nano, Castrone, Androgyno

They are Volpone's unnatural family and embody the perverted nature of his desires of which they are the external representation. They also represent the unnatural standards and values which prevail in the comic world of *Volpone* until the end of the play.

Peregrine

Of all the characters in the play Peregrine is the only one whom Jonson presents uncritically. His name means 'falcon' or 'traveller'. The falcon is in obvious contrast with the parrot represented by 'Sir Pol' who merely parrots the opinion of others. The falcon is a noble bird and Peregrine is both a gentleman and a wit. In the play he represents good judgement and normality and he shows up the pretentious absurdity of Sir Politic Would-Be. He also has a sense of humour which he puts to a good use when he determines to reveal Sir Politic's foolishness to him. Both Celia and Bonario seem rather humourless in comparison to Peregrine. It is Peregrine's relationship with Sir Politic which forms the comic sub-plot of the play.

Sir Politic Would-Be

Sir Politic is the most absurd character of the play, as his nickname 'Sir Pol' indicates. It also suggests his habit of repeating the opinions of others. The legacy hunters are given the names of birds of prey or carrion feeders, Peregrine the name of a noble bird of prey, but Sir Politic is inevitably associated in the audience's mind with the foolish parrot, despite his pretence of being a knowledgeable and experienced traveller. His name, 'Politic Would-Be', also indicates his striving for a cunning of which he is incapable. From his opening speech, with its unconscious abuse of language, Sir Politic is presented as a figure of fun. Like his wife, he does not always manage to say what he means. He also takes an unhealthy interest in his own excretory functions, which is revealed to the audience when Peregrine reads from his journal. Sir Politic, like Volpone in the main plot, whose double in this sense he is, is full of schemes for making money. The difference is that Sir Politic's schemes are all harebrained and harmless, whereas Volpone depends on fraud and deception and end by frustrating people's hopes.

Like his wife's, his mind is full of trivia and what he actually says constantly undermines his pretence of being an experienced man of the world. He is in fact the most gullible character in the play, as Peregrine demonstrates to him, when he manages to persuade him to disguise himself as a giant tortoise to avoid arrest. But Sir Pol learns from his experience and determines to leave Venice. He is, indeed, the only character in the play who developes and becomes wiser.

5.2 IMAGERY

Jonson's use of figurative language contributes significantly to the meanings to be found in the play. There has been a good deal of exploration of Shakespearean imagery, but apart from Partridge's study *The Broken Compass*, comparatively little of Ben Jonson's metaphorical language. An examination of the imagery of *Volpone* under different headings reveals additional meanings which might otherwise be ignored.

Gold Imagery

Gold is the central symbol of the play and a great many references are made to it. To Volpone himself it is the highest good, and he addresses it in the language of religious devotion in his opening speech. Throughout the play it is valued more highly than people. When Mosca wants to tempt Volpone with Celia's beauty he describes her in terms of gold; she is:

> Bright as your gold! and lovely as your gold! (I.v. 114)

When the radiance and loveliness of a beautiful woman are compared to an inert metal there is a reification effect and she is reduced to an object. This occurs in the many places, where Celia is treated as a commodity that can be bought and sold. Volpone believes that gold can purchase love, for when he has seen Celia for the first time he tells Mosca:

> . . . Mosca, take my keys,
> Gold, plate, and jewels . . . nay, coin me, too,
> So thou, in this, but crown my longings. (II.iv. 21–4)

When Volpone desires Celia he expresses his longings in terms of money. As previously mentioned, love and money are interchangeable for Volpone.

In the corrupt world of the play gold is the supreme good. Even Lady Would-Be, when she makes her verbal slip, refers to the 'golden mediocrity'. Corvino is prepared to prostitute his wife Celia for it and the language he uses to describe this act includes a metaphor in which Celia is likened to the precious metal:

> . . . What is my gold
> The worse, for touching? (III.vii. 40–41)

When left alone with Celia Volpone leaps up from his couch and offers her material objects in the belief that he can buy her. But above all he offers her gold, and even proposes that they should drink it:

Our drink shall be prepared gold and amber (III.vii. 217)

It is left to Bonario to reveal the unnatural and unreal value of this most precious of metals, when he appears from hiding to rescue Celia and calls Volpone's gold 'this dross, thy idol'. The repeated references to it throughout the play give gold a symbolic value. It represents the unnatural values of Volpone as opposed to the human values represented by Celia and Bonario. At the time that Jonson was writing there was an enormous impact on the European economy from the gold arriving from the newly discovered Americas, which some historians have seen as one of the factors which pushed Europe towards capitalism.

Animal Imagery

Another group of images which is important in the play is the imagery associated with birds of prey and predatory animals, applied to the legacy hunters and to Volpone himself. In I.ii Volpone describes them thus:

> Now, now, my clients
> Begin their visitation! vulture, kite,
> Raven and gor-crow, all my birds of prey. (I.ii. 88–90)

The use of these comparisons is also emphasised to the audience through their names: Voltore, Corbaccio, Corvino. Strictly speaking they are not in fact birds of prey, but birds which feed on carrion: dead matter. This is even more appropriate when we remember that it is Volpone's dead body which they hope to feed on and profit by.
   Throughout the play people are reduced to the level of animals and Volpone often thinks of himself as his namesake, the fox, as when he refers to Aesop's fable of the fox and the crow:

> . . . Good! and not a fox
> Stretched on the earth, with fine delusive sleights,
> Mocking a gaping crow? (I.ii. 95–7)

A doctor is given the name of a wolf – the most feared of European predators:

> MOSCA   Yes, Signior Lupo, the physician (II.vi. 61)

In the first court-room scene, where Bonario and Celia are falsely accused, the references to animals increase, but they are applied by the guilty to the innocent Bonario and Celia. Corbaccio addresses his own son, Bonario, thus:

> I will not hear thee,
> Monster of men, swine, goat, wolf, parricide,
> Speak not, thou viper. (IV.v. 110–12)

Even Lady Would-Be addresses Celia in this way:

> Out, thou chameleon harlot! Now thine eyes
> Vie tears with the hyena! (IV.vi. 2–3)

The frequency of the references makes this scene sound like a list of the animals found most unpleasant by man.

When Volpone arranges for Mosca to announce his death he predicts how the legacy hunters will behave:

> I shall have instantly my vulture, crow,
> Raven, come flying hither on the news,
> To peck for carrion, my she-wolf and all
> Greedy, and full of expectation . . . (V.ii. 64–7)

and he refers to the exact details of the fable by Aesop, on which the allegorical level of the play is based, when he again identifies himself with the fox:

> A witty merchant, the fine bird, Corvino,
> That have such moral emblems on your name,
> Should not have sung your shame, and dropped your cheese,
> To let the Fox laugh at your emptiness. (V.viii. 11–14)

But it is Mosca who is compared to the lowest form of life when Voltore compares him to a blow-fly which feeds on dead and decaying matter:

> VOLTORE Well, flesh-fly, it is summer with you now;
> Your winter will come on. (V.ix. 1)

The animal imagery in the play functions in several ways. The most important of these is to suggest the debased natures of the legacy hunters and Mosca. Jonson's attitude to Volpone is ambivalent. The fox is a more admirable creature both in fact and in fable, famous for his cunning. The animal imagery also suggests that the play works on an allegorical level, with Volpone as the fox cheating the carrion-eaters by pretending to be dead.

Feeding Imagery

Edward Partridge, the critic who made the pioneering study of
Jonson's use of imagery in his book *The Broken Compass*, believes
that the feeding imagery is the central imagery of *Volpone*. Whether
we agree with this view or not, it is certainly one of the most
important groups of images in the play. It is expressed in the
predatory behaviour of the legacy hunters and by Volpone himself in
his attempted seduction of Celia, when he promises her all his wealth
but describes it in terms of feeding:

> . . . See, behold,
> What thou art queen of; not in expectation,
> As I feed others, but possessed, and crowned. (III.vii. 188–90)

The greed of the legacy hunters for gold assumes the dimensions of
a physical need for food and this is suggested by their names and the
imagery of predatory animals which surround them. Mosca's chosen
vocation of parasite is defined in the Shorter Oxford English Dictionary as 'one who eats at the expense of another'. The feeding imagery
is completed in the final scene, when the guilty are punished and the
first advocate says:

> . . . Mischiefs feed
> Like beasts, till they be fat, and then they bleed. (V.xii. 150–1)

Imagery of Sickness and Decay

One of the central metaphors of the play is that of sickness, death and
corruption. Volpone pretends to be sick and much of the imagery
surrounding him is of sickness and decay. This is expanded to the
whole city of Venice at one point, which is likewise portrayed as
decayed and diseased:

> . . . it was, in Volpone's time,
> Your predecessor, ere he grew diseased,
> A handsome, pretty, customed bawdy-house
> As any was in Venice (none dispraised)
> But fell with him; his body and that house
> Decayed together. (V.vii. 10–14)

There is also the suggestion of venereal disease and bubonic plague
when Mosca curses Volpone in his attempt to incite Corvino to do the
same:

MOSCA   The pox approach and add to your diseases . . .
. . . and the plague to boot. (I.v. 52–5)

Imagery of Discharge

The sense of corruption and disease in the play is partly created by
the number of images concerned with unpleasant discharges which
occur in it. This is particularly so in the scenes where Volpone
appears on his sick-bed, as when Mosca describes Volpone's symptoms to Corbaccio:

> MOSCA   Yes, sir, and from his brain—
> CORBACCIO   I conceive you good,
> MOSCA   Flows a cold sweat, with a continual rheum,
> Forth the resolved corners of his eyes. (I.iv. 47–9)

'Rheum' is a watery matter discharged from the nose, eyes or mouth.
This series of disagreeable images reaches its apotheosis in I.v, where
Mosca encourages Corvino to insult Volpone to his face by pretend-
ing that he is deaf:

> MOSCA   Those filthy eyes of yours, that flow with slime
> Like two frog-pits . . .
> CORVINO   His nose is like a common sewer, still running.
> MOSCA   'Tis good! And what his mouth?
> CORVINO   A very draught. (I.v. 56–66)

The crescendo of excremental imagery reaches its climax with the
word 'draught', which meant 'cesspool.' The effect of this imagery is
to indicate the decadent, decaying and unhealthy nature of Volpone.
The malodorous imagery adds to the sense of putrefaction and
Jonson even descends to the scatological. The final result of feeding is
of course excretion. Jonson thereby reminds us of the animal nature
of man.

Study of the play's imagery increases our appreciation of the text
and indicates possible critical approaches to it. Jonson's use of
metaphorical language is significant. The imagery of gold, animals,
feeding, sickness, decay and discharge all contribute to the meaning.
The images are an integral part of the play and their function is not
just ornamental.

5.3   LANGUAGE

Jonson was master of a great number of styles, from the elevated to
the scatological. The only modern writer who approaches Jonson in

this respect is James Joyce, who is also remarkable for his word-play and was, incidentally, a great admirer of Jonson's work. Like Shakespeare, Jonson studied the art of rhetoric at school and his work is full of a remarkable number of rhetorical devices. He makes particular use of paronomasia, or the pun, in which one word has two quite distinct meanings.

If we compare the speeches of Celia with those of Volpone in Act III scene vii, the seduction scene, we can begin to grasp the variety of Jonson's styles. Celia's speeches are remarkable for their Puritan plainness and absence of metaphor; Volpone's on the other hand are loaded with exotic images and hyperbole. The two styles are entirely appropriate for the two different characters and help their characterisation enormously.

Jonson's use of language also reflects the tremendous changes taking place in England in the seventeenth century with the rise of the middle class and the decline in importance of the monarchy and the aristocracy. Celia's speeches indicate the rising Puritan values of restraint, and Volpone's the declining aristocratic ones of ostentatious display. In the seventeenth century there was an attempt to reform the English language, started by Francis Bacon and carried on by the Royal Society, to avoid the use of metaphor and to encourage the use of a pure plain style. This was part of the Puritan project to establish their values and which led to the growth of science and to the rise of capitalism in England.

Jonson was also capable of great verbal exuberance. If we look at Volpone's speech in II.ii, where he is disguised as Scoto, the use of language, with its mixture of scatological verbal jokes in the manner of Aristophanes, together with its derogatory tone, is unique to Jonson among English dramatists. As mentioned before Jonson had a remarkable aptitude for invective and here he demonstrates a breathtaking use of scurrilous language. Most of the play is written in blank verse, but in the speeches of Volpone (disguised as Scoto) Jonson convincingly shows his mastery of prose in order to convey the manner of delivery of the huckster:

Those turdy-facy-nasty-paty-lousy-fartical rogues. (II.ii. 61)

Jonson invents the portmanteau word 'fartical'. It is a compound word made up of 'farcical' and 'fart', which condenses the two meanings to suggest Volpone's view of the other mountebanks. Because of the wit and inventiveness that Jonson uses, the audience laughs at this scatological language as the series of adjectives crowd upon each other.

It is worth noticing Jonson's use of the pun as a comic device. If, as Aristotle said, tragedy portrays men as better than they are, while comedy portrays them as worse, then Jonson's scatological use of the pun both undermines his characters' pretensions and reminds the audience of man's animal and physical nature. Sir Politic Would-Be's wish to be considered an experienced man of the world is continually subverted by the unconscious puns he keeps making in his speech in II.i:

> Sir, to a wise man, all the world's his soil.

The surface meaning of 'soil' is subverted by its hidden and secondary meaning of excrement. So with one word Jonson punctures the pretentiousness of Sir Politic and shows the audience that he is to be perceived as a comic character.

Jonson brilliantly uses language in speeches which not only dramatise the characters and advance the action of the play but also surprise the audience with their virtuosity; however, he never uses this ability merely to amaze the audience, but always harnesses it to his dramatic purpose. The kind of verbal profusion and use of metaphorical language found in Elizabethan and Jacobean writing was eventually to disappear from the language, to be replaced by a plainer and more exact use of English. By the eighteenth century modern English prose had evolved, with its stress on clarity rather than effect.

5.4 SETTING

Jonson's setting for the play is no accident. For a seventeenth-century English audience Italy was a dangerous and exotic place. There was great suspicion of Catholics and Catholicism. The Gunpowder Plot had taken place in 1605, just a year before *Volpone*'s first performance. Italy was also famous in England for producing Machiavelli, the author of *The Prince*, whose principle of political expediency became in the English popular imagination the embodiment of unscrupulous and cunning evil, in the figure of the Machiavellian, who appeared on the English stage as a character in many plays. The most famous example is Iago in Shakespeare's *Othello*.

Venice had long ago risen to maritime prominence. It controlled the Eastern Mediterranean and the European trading ports of the Byzantine Empire. Although somewhat fallen from its former pre-eminence the republic was still famous for its wealth and its skill at trade. Venice was a convenient symbol for Jonson of the corruption which is the subject of *Volpone*. There was great curiosity about the rest of Europe in England and as foreign travel was arduous and difficult there was a great vogue for travellers' accounts of their experiences in Europe. Many such accounts were published in the

late sixteenth and early seventeenth century, as well as such fictiona-
lised ones as Thomas Nashe's *The Unfortunate Traveller*. This
describes the misfortunes suffered by the Englishman abroad and
parts of it may have influenced Jonson when he came to write
Volpone. The advice given by Sir Politic Would-Be to Peregrine
could have been borrowed straight from this book: 'Beleeve nothing,
trust no man, yet seemed thou as thou swallowedest all, suspectedst
none, but wert easie to be gulled by everie one.' (*The Unfortunate
Traveller*).

In particular Italy was famous for plots. The hero of *The Unfortunate Traveller*, Jack Wilton, narrowly escapes being executed for a
crime he has not committed. He meets a banished and disillusioned
earl whose advice to Jack is to stay at home in England, for the effect
of Italy on the young traveller is not beneficial: 'From there he brings
the art of atheisme, the art of epicurising, the art of whoring, the art
of poysoning . . . ' (*The Unfortunate Traveller*). These remarks give
some idea of how the average Englishman perceived Italy at the time.

The contemporary account of foreign travel with which *Volpone*
has most affinities is *Coryate's Crudities*. It seems reasonable to
assume Jonson's familiarity with it before its publication because he
wrote some of the couplets to its illustrations. The aspects of Venice
Jonson alludes to in the play are the same as those described by
Coryate. The features of Venice which Coryate describes include the
mountebanks for which Venice was famous, the close watch kept by
Venetian husbands over their wives, the charms of the Venetian
courtesans, and even the sale of tortoises in the market.

5.5 DIVISION INTO ACTS

After the prologue, where he indicates his dramatic methods and
purpose, Jonson casts his play in the five-act form: *Act I* introduces us
to the main action involving Volpone, Mosca and the legacy seekers.
Act II brings in the sub-plot involving Sir Politic and Lady Would-Be.
Act III introduces the complication of Bonario's intervention in the
action after he has overheard Volpone's attempted seduction of
Celia. *Act IV* reaches a false conclusion when Bonario and Celia are
found guilty by the court because Corvino, Corbaccio, and Lady
Would-Be have committed perjury, and made false allegations
against them. *Act V* provides the resolution and the true conclusion
when Volpone and Mosca fall out and Volpone reveals the truth to
the court.

5.6 THE UNITIES

Time

Jonson observes the unity of time. The action of Volpone takes place
in one day. The play opens with the sunrise and Volpone's salutation
to the sun and his gold, and ends in the evening with him receiving his
sentence at the hands of the court.

Place

Jonson also observes the unity of place. All the action takes place in
Venice, although in different locations.

Action

Jonson does not observe the unity of action because he introduces the
sub-plot. This does not detract from the effectiveness of the play,
because it acts as a commentary and a counterpoint to the main
action and provides comic relief.

5.7 NOTES ON PRODUCING THE PLAY

Like Shakespeare, Jonson was an experienced actor and knew what
would work on the stage. However, there are several problems which
confront the contemporary producer of *Volpone*, not least of these its
extreme length. A production of the complete play would take at
least four hours to perform, and a present-day audience, whose
viewing habits are formed primarily by television and the cinema, has
an attention span considerably shorter than its Elizabethan and
Jacobean predecessors. Most modern productions have got round
this by cutting out the sub-plot, the simplest means of shortening the
play. But this must inevitably diminish the play's effect, as the
sub-plot conveys an important part of the meaning and is an ironic
counterpart of the main plot. There has been at least one fairly recent
performance of *Volpone*, almost in its entirety, complete with
sub-plot, namely, Tyrone Guthrie's production for the National
Theatre in 1968, which is generally considered to have been the most
successful production of it mounted in the twentieth century.

  A question which must also exercise the mind of the producer is to
what extent he is to allow the language and imagery to influence how
he stages the play. There are obvious hints as to the appearance of
the costumes of the various characters in the imagery of predatory

animals, with Volpone as the fox and the suitors as different birds of carrion. Tyrone Guthrie's production took the animal caricatures into account both in the costumes and in the performances of the actors.

Another problem which inevitably confronts the producer of an Elizabethan or Jacobean play is the period in which to set it. Shakespeare's plays have been successfully performed both in modern dress and set in other periods, but producers of *Volpone* have tended to set it in its own period. There is the obvious advantage of simplicity in this, but it would be interesting to see a production in modern dress in order to gain a new perspective on the play.

The contemporary actor invariably fails to give sufficient weight to the fact that he is speaking dramatic verse. This is largely due to the supremacy of the realistic style of acting brought about by the demands of a mainly realistic theatre, cinematic realism, and a more intimate acting style encouraged by the use of the close-up. Consequently the actor is nervous when called upon to speak Elizabethan dramatic poetry. It has been difficult to tell from many recent Shakespearean productions that Shakespeare actually wrote in verse, as the actors tend to speak his lines as if they were prose, ignoring the rhythms and flattening the poetry. Jonson's verse, like Marlowe's, cries out to be declaimed, and no more is this so than in Volpone's opening speech. The Elizabethan theatre was more stylised than our own and ideally this should be reflected in the delivery of the lines in such a way as not to diminish the poetry. Volpone is not a realistic play in the sense of twentieth-century realistic theatre, although the characterisation would have been acceptable to its original audience, and the characters must be portrayed on stage as larger than life. Some stylisation is therefore inevitable and necessary, both in the performances of the actors, and in the way that they speak their lines. Poetry, after all, is heightened language using all its resources and resonances.

In *Volpone* Jonson created parts that the actor can get his teeth into. The central character offers the actor taking his part golden opportunities. He is a monstrous egotist and there are many indications in the text for developing his character, not only in interaction with the other dramatis personae, but particularly in his soliloquies where he reveals his innermost feelings to the audience. The part of Mosca, likewise, offers much scope to the actor playing him. The truly comic figures of the piece are Sir Politic and Lady Would-Be and they have many chances to make the audience laugh. The dialogue given to Sir Politic characterises him as an eccentric and foolish Englishman of a type familiar at the time, and even today, while Lady Would-Be, his wife, is also supremely comic with her garrulousness and slips of the tongue together with her obsessive concern with her appearance, and her desire to show off as much of her body as possible. All these give clues to the actor in search of a character. Even the minor characters are carefully drawn, with idiosyncrasies that make them believable and individual.

The play on the stage, therefore, reminds us of what we tend to forget if we only study the play as a text. It is extremely funny. *Volpone* is one of the great comedies in the English language, with its satire and rapidity of action. It is almost farce-like with the large number of incidents which crowd upon each other, and the unpredictability of its plot. An important factor for the producer and the actors is that a rapid pace is required, not in the delivery of the lines, for many of these must be played for laughs, but in the picking up of cues. There are many touches which contribute to the success of the play on the stage. Among these are Jonson's use of specifically theatrical devices. He uses the aside as a humorous commentary on the action when Mosca reveals the true thoughts of Volpone and the legacy hunters. He shows a sure dramatic touch when he deepens the mood in the first scene of the fifth, and final act, with Volpone's soliloquy on disease, old age and death. He creates dramatic conflict in the central confrontation between Vice and Virtue in the figures of Volpone and Celia. Finally, he sustains the dramatic tension and the audience's uncertainty about the outcome until the final dénouement, which comes with the unexpected unmasking of Volpone, and which communicates that element of surprise and release which is the essence of theatre. These are a few of the supreme theatrical moments which occur in the play and help to make it the dramatic masterwork it is. Jonson's development of his complicated plot and his use of the five-act form is masterly. Of particular note is the way he uses the sub-plot to highlight the main action, and his use of complication, false conclusion and final resolution in the main plot.

The language used by his characters is carefully chosen. One of his avowed aims was to write in 'language such as men do use' and he creates an impression of the ordinary speech of his time, even though many of the central speeches of the play show careful construction and a dazzling use of rhetorical devices and poetic figures. Jonson's command of language and dramatic dialogue mean that in his masterpiece *Volpone* the characters are believable and supremely actable, so that he achieved what he stated to be his aim in his Prologue to *Every Man In His Humour*:

> But deeds, and language, such as men do use,
> And persons, such as Comedy would choose,
> When she would show an image of the times. (21–3)

6 CRITICAL EXAMINATION
OF A PASSAGE

VOLPONE   Good morning to the day; and, next, my gold!
Open the shrine, that I may see my saint.
(MOSCA *reveals the treasure*)
Hail the world's soul, and mine! More glad than is
The teeming earth to see the longed-for sun
Peep through the horns of the celestial Ram,
Am I, to view thy splendour, darkening his;
That, lying here, amongst my other hoards,
Show'st like a flame by night; or like the day
Struck out of Chaos, when all darkness fled
Unto the centre. O, thou son of Sol
(But brighter than thy father) let me kiss,
With adoration, thee, and every relic
Of sacred treasure in this blessed room.
Well did wise poets by thy glorious name
Title that age which they would have the best,
Thou being the best of things – and far transcending
All style of joy, in children, parents, friends,
Or any other waking dream on earth.
Thy looks, when they to Venus did ascribe,
They should have given her twenty thousand Cupids;
Such are thy beauties, and our loves! Dear saint,
Riches, the dumb god that giv'st all men tongues;
That canst do naught, and yet mak'st men do all things;
The price of souls; even hell, with thee to boot,
Is made worth heaven! Thou art virtue, fame,
Honour, and all things else! Who can get thee,
He shall be noble, valiant, honest, wise . . . (I.i. 1–27)

The opening speech of the play is a eulogy – a speech in praise of gold, and it introduces us to Volpone's personal sphere where the professed standards of civilisation do not apply; it also indicates how we are intended to perceive the central character. The playwright adopts Marlowe's use of blank verse, written in iambic pentameters, and also his declamatory style as, in ringing lines reminiscent of Barabas's speeches in the *Jew of Malta*, Volpone greets the day.

The audience is startled to hear him address his treasure as if it were a god or saint, with the dramatist's skilful use of a rhetorical device called apostrophe, which consists of addressing an inanimate object as if it were alive and capable of understanding. The audience is also surprised to hear it described in language more usually applied to religious devotion. Much of the force of these lines and the rest of the speech derives from this exchange of contexts, that of religious worship and gold, a common symbol for crass materialism even today. The most familiar use of this metaphorical exchange of contexts is in love poetry, where the beloved is addressed in language more appropriate for sacred love than profane. A contemporary and friend of Jonson, John Donne, frequently used religious imagery in his love poetry and erotic imagery in his religious poetry. This creates a sense of shock in the reader. In Jonson's case the shock is even greater in that the religious is mixed with the materialistic in an unprecedented and unfamiliar way.

The reader is struck by the directness with which Jonson attacks the main theme of the play, and without more ado introduces us both to the central character and his obsession. The opening line is balanced and antithetical; the close juxtaposition of the greeting to the day and then the gold is masterfully employed by Jonson to begin the series of comparisons between gold and light which occur through the first ten lines of the play. After beginning on a note of salutation to the day, the second half of the line rapidly descends to the real subject of the speech. Jonson maintains the elevated tone in the next line, now likening gold to a saint, as Volpone commands Mosca to reveal his treasure.

When Mosca has done this, Jonson raises the stylistic level even higher, to that of a panegyric or address of formal praise. He skilfully employs rhetorical devices for his own ends, appropriating them from their more traditional use and using them for comic effect. His enterprise throughout this speech is to make Volpone's love of the precious metal appear ridiculous. Jonson's intended meaning constantly works against the ostensible or surface meaning, undermining it and subverting it.

> Hail the world's soul, and mine! More glad than is
> The teeming earth to see the longed-for sun
> Peep through the horns of the celestial Ram,

> Am I, to view thy splendour, darkening his;
> That, lying here, amongst my other hoards,
> Show'st like a flame by night; or like the day
> Struck out of Chaos, when all darkness fled
> Unto the centre. (3–10)

With extreme exaggeration Volpone addresses his plunder as the soul of the world. In classical times this was supposed to be the animating principle of matter, the source of all life on earth. In this comparison and in the next line Volpone is paradoxically suggesting by association that gold has the power to create life, whereas in fact it is an inert metal. Note the use of 'teeming earth', which suggests the boundless fertility of the earth in spring. The metaphor, drawn from astrology, tells us it is spring time, when the sun enters the sign of Aries. This adds to the suggestion of new life and growth after winter. But the final effect is one of sterility, because Volpone is talking about his joy at seeing his wealth.

Not content with this absurd exaggeration, he now makes the most extreme series of comparisons of the speech. First he states that his booty darkens the sun, then he describes it as a 'flame by night', continuing the imagery of light to which gold is compared. Finally, in the most outrageous comparison of the passage, he compares his hoard to the act of Creation, when, according to Greek mythology, Day was created out of Chaos and Night. The speech progresses by a series of hyperboles or exaggerated statements, which lead on from one to the next. The effect is both startling and comic. Love of wealth is not in itself an amusing subject, but when this love of riches is pursued to the extent that it becomes a religion, then we become aware of the unnaturalness of the emotion. It is upon this imaginative inflation of a common and petty human emotion, until it reaches absurd proportions, that Jonson's satire relies.

> O, thou son of Sol
> (But brighter than thy father) let me kiss,
> With adoration, thee, and every relic
> Of sacred treasure in this blessed room (10–14)

In another apostrophe Volpone addresses his bullion as 'son of Sol', suggesting that it is a child of the sun. (The alchemists believed that gold was born from the sun.) But he immediately qualifies this by saying that he is brighter than his father. There is also a pun on 'Sol' because a 'sol' was a French coin worth one twentieth of a livre. Moving from the comparison of his gold to the sun, he now likens it to a holy relic, which was usually some part of a saint's body, venerated by pious Christians. The language used is that of religious fervour: 'adoration', 'sacred' and 'blessed'. With the last two adject-

ives Volpone demonstrates that he has raised his greed to the level of
religious devotion.

> Well did wise poets by thy glorious name
> Title that age which they would have the best,
> Thou being the best of things . . . 14–16)

The speech looks back to classical times when Greek and Roman
poets dreamed of a happy former time which they called 'the golden
age'. Gold's very name means the best and it is the 'best of things'.

> and far transcending
> All style of joy, in children, parents, friends (16–17)

Continuing his argument that gold is the highest good, Volpone next
states that its pleasures are higher than all human love. The unnaturalness of Volpone's love of gold is shown most clearly here. His love
of it has displaced normal human affection, and he has created an
unnatural family for himself, composed of a dwarf, a hermaphrodite
and a eunuch. Even his closest associate, the person in the play who
comes closest to being a friend, Mosca, is bought, his friendship
purchased with gifts of money. Jonson's moral point of view, which is
always implied, comes across most strongly here. All of Volpone's
relationships are based on money and are worthless.

> Thy looks, when they to Venus did ascribe,
> They should have given her twenty thousand Cupids;
> Such are thy beauties, and our loves! Dear saint,
> Riches, the dumb god that giv'st all men tongues;
> That canst do naught, and yet mak'st men do all things;
> The price of souls; even hell, with thee to boot,
> Is made worth heaven! Thou art virtue, fame,
> Honour, and all things else! Who can get thee,
> He shall be noble, valiant, honest, wise . . . (19–27)

Referring back to the 'wise poets' Volpone now says that they should
have given Venus 'twenty thousand Cupids' when they attributed the
beauty of gold to her. This intricate and ingenious comparison of the
beauty of gold to the goddess from classical mythology is further
extended to include her son Cupid. The suggestion is that, like gold,
Venus should have been given the ability to multiply herself a
thousand times. Jonson's use of imagery drawn from classical sources
is both exact and witty.

Then, once again, he uses the language of religious adoration to
address his loot in another apostrophe which is extended to the end of
the speech: 'Dear saint . . . ' Wittily Jonson describes gold as a

'dumb gold that giv'st all men tongues', referring to gold's power to loosen men's tongues and make them talk. He next refers to gold's power to make men do things even though in itself it is inert:

> That canst do naught, and yet mak'st men do all things. (23)

In an outrageous blasphemy gold is even given the same power as the blood of Christ: to purchase men's souls. To Jonson's original audience such a sentiment would have been sacrilegious, as would the suggestion that gold can convert hell to heaven. Jonson is setting out to shock his audience and he does:

> The price of souls; even hell, with thee to boot,
> Is made worth heaven! (24–5)

Finally gold is equated with all human virtues. (That is because people attribute all the virtues to a wealthy man.):

> Thou art virtue, fame,
> Honour, and all things else! Who can get thee,
> He shall be noble, valiant, honest, wise . . . (25–7)

The outrageousness of Volpone's speech lies in the variance between the values stated in it compared to the received ones. (When Jonson was writing, feudal values were changing to those of a money economy.) By raising greed and acquisitiveness to the level of a religion Jonson succeeds in making it appear ridiculous and laughable. And yet he was not the first writer to employ such means to satirise greed. According to the scholar Coburn Gum, the ancient Greek writer Aristophanes employed a similar device in his play *Plutus*, which Jonson borrowed. Here, Plutus the Greek god of wealth is the real ruler of the world, not Zeus, and wealth is worshipped as a deity. Legacy hunting had also been made the subject of satire by such Roman writers as Juvenal, Horace and Petronius.

This is not to belittle Jonson's achievement, but to place it in perspective. His reading of the classics made an indelible impression on him and he returns to them time and time again in his writing, as a source of inspiration. His skill and lightness of touch in using the classical authors is remarkable. There is no sense of pedantic knowledge being laboriously unpacked: his sources are skilfully woven into the fabric of the play. Renaissance writers did not have our post-Romantic craving for originality. Shakespeare, for example, copied nearly all the plots for his plays from other works. Jonson was proud of his learning and considered that

> For a man to write well, there are three necessaries – to read the best authors, to observe the best speakers, and much exercise of his own style. (*Timber*, 115).

The opening speech of the play introduces us to Volpone's unreal world and the values that prevail there. Through the use of hyperbole and comic exaggeration the audience is shown how ridiculous his religion of gold is. The speech prepares the audience for the play, indicating Jonson's satiric intention, and how Volpone is to be perceived. Brilliantly, Jonson plunges the audience directly into the play and the psychology of the main character.

Jonson's use of language shows a Renaissance energy and exuberance and is encrusted with images. Never before or since that time has the English language been so metaphorical. The imagery employed in the speech is drawn from many and varied sources. Jonson ransacks the classical authors, astrology, religion and alchemy to produce the gaudy imagery of the speech which over-inflates the importance of gold. Later English satirists, Dryden and Pope, were to follow Jonson's example and create effective satire by elevating an unworthy subject so that it appears comic and ultimately ridiculous.

7 CRITICAL RECEPTION

Jonson's treatment at the hands of the critics has not always been just. He has all too often been compared disparagingly with Shakespeare, his great contemporary. In his lifetime Jonson's reputation stood high, and even in the century after his death Dryden praised his work, calling him 'the greatest man of the last age'. But in the nineteenth century, particularly among Romantic critics who were out of sympathy with Jonson's aims and methods, his work was compared unfavourably with Shakespeare. One of the few who came to a just assessment of Jonson's achievement was the poet Coleridge who considered 'The Fox to be the greatest of Ben Jonson's works', and wrote:

> Ben Jonson is original; he is, indeed, the only one of the great dramatists of the day who was not either directly produced or very greatly modified by Shakespeare.
> (*Lectures and Notes on Shakespeare and other English poets*)

He had this to say of Jonson's characterisation:

> The characters in his plays are, in the strictest sense of the term, abstractions. Some very prominent feature is taken from the whole man, and that single feature or humour is made the basis upon which the entire character is built up. (Ibid.)

But it is his comments on Jonson's style which carry most weight:

> Ben Jonson exhibits a sterling English diction, and he has with great skill contrived varieties of construction; but his style is rarely sweet and harmonious, in consequence of his labour at point and strength being so evident. (Ibid.)

Coleridge also thought highly of Jonson's plots:

> Indeed I ought very particularly to call your attention to the
> extraordinary skill shown by Ben Jonson in contriving situations
> for the display of his characters. In fact, his care and anxiety in
> this matter led him to do what scarcely any of the dramatists of
> the age did – that is, invent his plots. (Ibid.)

T. S. Eliot began the revival of Jonson's critical fortunes in the
twentieth century with his essay entitled 'Ben Jonson', in which he
says of *Volpone*:

> The plot does not hold the play together; what holds the play
> together is a unity of inspiration that radiates into plot and
> personage alike. ('Ben Jonson', T. S. Eliot, repr. in *Ben Jonson:
> A Collection of Critical Essays*)

He says of Jonson's satiric method:

> But satire like Jonson's is great in the end not by hitting off its
> object, but by creating it . . .

Like Coleridge he comments on Jonson's characterisation:

> . . . it is an art of caricature, of great caricature, like Marlowe's.

After T. S. Eliot's reappreciation, Jonson's work began to be taken
more seriously, and a number of excellent studies appeared. The
literary critic L. C. Knights, one of the pioneers in twentieth-century
Jonson criticism, sees greed as the subject of *Volpone*:

> The greed that forms the subject of *Volpone* includes both the
> desire of sensuous pleasure as an end in itself, and the desire for
> riches. (*Drama and Society in the Age of Jonson*, repr. in
> *Volpone*, Casebook Series, pp.78–87)

He also finds an anti-acquisitive attitude informed by the traditional
economic morality of the Middle Ages:

> It is this anti-acquisitive attitude which reaches its fullest expres-
> sion in *Volpone*. (Ibid.)

The American critic, Edmund Wilson, gave a Freudian reading of
Volpone in his book *The Triple Thinkers*. Although negative and
hostile in his approach, both to Jonson and the play, he makes some
interesting points. He describes Jonson and his character Volpone as
anal erotic types:

The point is that Ben Jonson depends on the exhibition of stored away knowledge to compel admiration by itself. And the hoarding and withholding of money is the whole subject of that strange play *Volpone*. ('Morose Ben Jonson' in *Ben Jonson: A Collection of Critical Essays*, p.64)

He also comments on the fact that Volpone gets pleasure not just from hoarding his gold but also:

> from stimulating others to desire it, to hope to inherit it from him, and then frustrating them with the gratuitous cruelty which has been noted as one of the features of the aggressive side of this Freudian type. (Ibid. p.65)

A more recent critic, Edward B. Partridge, in his book *The Broken Compass* made the first systematic study of Jonson's use of imagery in his comedies. He identifies several kinds of imagery in *Volpone*: religious imagery, classical and erotic imagery, and finally the imagery of feeding which he thinks is the central imagery in the play:

> Feeding might be said to symbolise the double theme of greed for riches and lust for sensuous pleasures. One might call it the central image of the play because it is the core of many other images. (Edward B. Partridge, *The Broken Compass* repr. in *Volpone*, Casebook Series, p.151)

One of the most interesting recent discoveries has been the extent to which Jonson was influenced by the ancient Greek playwright Aristophanes. In his book *The Aristophanic Comedies of Ben Jonson*, Coburn Gum has proved that Jonson was indebted to Aristophanes and Greek Old Comedy for his fixed characters, his creation of a 'topsy-turvy world' and even his 'indecency and obscenity'. Jonson's introductions to his plays, which to a modern audience might seem intrusive, were also based on the Aristophanic model.

> To develop his satire, and to establish rapport between himself and his audience, the poet of Old Comedy used extra-dramatic intrusions, called parabases. Such devices broke the theatrical illusion, and permitted the playwright to address the spectators directly. (Coburn Gum, *The Aristophanic Comedies of Ben Jonson*, p. 17)

Volpone is the one play by Jonson about which a significant body of criticism has grown. The twentieth century has seen the rescue of Jonson from his undeserved obscurity and his introduction to a wider audience. The above selection of quotations from the critics is by no means exhaustive, but represents some of the most important points of view about Ben Jonson and his play *Volpone*.

REVISION QUESTIONS

1. Is *Volpone* a tragi-comedy?
2. What significance does gold have in the play?
3. Discuss Jonson's use of satire in *Volpone*.
4. Analyse and discuss the relationship between the 'gulls' and the 'knaves'.
5. *Volpone* attacks many human weaknesses. What values are implied in the play?
6. Describe and discuss Jonson's use of language in *Volpone*.
7. Discuss the play's imagery.
8. Comment on the view that the subject of *Volpone* is greed.
9. Describe the relationship between Volpone and Mosca.
10. To what extent is *Volpone* about disease and death?
11. Discuss the significance of the sub-plot.
12. To what extent do you think that Jonson's characters are one-dimensional?

FURTHER READING

Armstrong, W., 'Ben Jonson and Jacobean Stagecraft', in J. Russell Brown and Bernard Harris (eds.) *The Jacobean Theatre* (London: Arnold, 1960).

Barish, Jonas A. *Ben Jonson and the Language of Prose Comedy* (Cambridge Mass: Harvard University Press, 1960).

Barish, Jonas A. (ed.), *Ben Jonson: A Collection of Critical Essays* (New Jersey: Prentice Hall, 1963).

Barish, Jonas A. (ed.), *Jonson Volpone a Casebook* (London: Macmillan, 1972).

Dick, Aliki Lafkidou, *Paedeia through Laughter* (The Hague: Mouton, 1974)

Gum, Coburn, *The Aristophanic Comedies of Ben Jonson* (The Hague: Mouton, 1969).

Herford, C. H., and Simpson, Percy, (eds.), *Ben Jonson*, 11 vols (Oxford: Clarendon Press, 1925–52).

Knights, L. C., *Drama and Society in the Age of Jonson* (London: Chatto and Windus 1937).

Knights, L. C., 'Ben Jonson Dramatist', in *The Age of Shakespeare* (London: Penguin Books, 1955).

Partridge, Edward B., *The Broken Compass: A Study of the Major Comedies of Ben Jonson* (London: Chatto and Windus, 1958).

Summers, Claude J. and Ted-Larry Pebworth, *Ben Jonson* (Boston: Twayne Publishers, 1979).